the girl's guide *to the* big bold moves for career success

HOW TO BUILD CONFIDENCE, CONQUER FEAR, MANAGE UP, NAVIGATE CHANGE AND MUCH, MUCH MORE

Caitlin Friedman
and Kimberly Yorio

BROADWAY BOOKS

new york

Formerly titled *The Girl's Guide to Kicking your Career into Gear*

BROADWAY

Copyright © 2008 by Caitlin Friedman and Kimberly Yorio

All Rights Reserved
Published in the United States by Broadway Books, an imprint of the Crown
Publishing Group, a division of Random House, Inc., New York.
www.crownpublishing.com

BROADWAY BOOKS and the Broadway Books colophon are trademarks of
Random House, Inc.

Originally published in hardcover in slightly different form in the United States as
The Girl's Guide to Kicking Your Career into Gear by Broadway Books, New York, in 2008.

Library of Congress Cataloging-in-Publication Data
Friedman, Caitlin.
The girl's guide to the big bold moves for career success / Caitlin Friedman and
Kimberly Yorio.
p. cm.
1. Vocational guidance for women. 2. Career development. I. Yorio, Kimberly.
II. Title.
HF5382.6.F74 2008
331.702082—dc22
2007022405

ISBN 978-0-7679-2767-3

Printed in the United States of America

Design by Caroline Cunningham

10 9 8 7 6 5 4 3 2 1

First Paperback Edition

Caitlin

> *For my best friend and best husband, Andrew,*
> *and my two joys, Declan and Taylor*

Kim

> *For Thomas*

contents

acknowledgments   vii

introduction   1

part one: make plans

one   you are here   5

two   getting where you want to go   27

part two: make contact

three   selling yourself (without selling out)   47

four   the new girl's network   66

part three: rise to the challenges

five   fear is a four-letter word   89

six   [insert stereotype here]   111

seven   change is often good   132

part four: think big

eight   running for (the corner) office   145

nine   big thinking   160

ten   asking for what you deserve   174

eleven   chick in charge   192

a final note   213

resources   221

index   223

acknowledgments

This book was definitely a group effort, so we have lots of people to thank for finally getting it on the bookshelves. Our agent, David Black, who continues to be our champion even while driving him crazy with idea #475. Our editor, Ann Campbell, who from Day One was as committed as we are to helping women think big about themselves in the workplace. Thanks to the publicity team at Broadway—our old friends David Drake and Tammy Blake and our new friend Tommy Semosh. Anne Watters for continuing the great marketing ideas. A shout out to the girls who get our books into stores all over the world, David Black's foreign-rights queens Susan Raihofer and Leigh Ann Eliseo. You know we love getting those offers from Croatia. We want to thank Tony Tackaberry at Lion Television for believing we could have a show. And we want to thank David Craig and Linda Berman at Media Nation for believing we could inspire a show. And we couldn't have written this book at all without Aimee Bianca and Gabriela Holdt holding down the fort at YC Media. Thanks, girls!

Kim has to thank her special group of girls who help wordsmith and wrangle interviews and generally cheerlead her through her life—Kara, Chrisi, Sharyn, Amy, Amie, and Laurice—you girls are the best.

Caitlin wants to thank Kim for being the best writing, business, speaking, and travel partner a girl could wish for. And Kim wants to thank Caitlin for continuing to come up with the big and small ideas that keep Girl's Guide exciting, fun, and the most rewarding professional venture of her life.

But the absolute biggest thank-you of all goes to all of those girls willing to share their stories, support Girl's Guide, and do what they can to help other women succeed.

introduction

ITE: three letters texting across cell phones everywhere. ITE (*in this economy*) as in "ITE, I can't go out for dinner tonight;" "ITE, I won't be getting a raise;" "ITE, I am worried about losing my job."

When we first published *The Girl's Guide to Kicking Your Career into Gear* in hardcover in January 2008, ITE wasn't in the lexicon. The economy was still strong, although for those who were looking, there were signs of bad things to come. We wrote this book as a guidebook for women to take charge of their worklives, so they can make more money and also create and nurture careers that will make them happy. Through research and interviews with hundreds of women across the country, we compiled lessons, strategies, and scores of success stories.

As the economy started declining and the news just kept getting worse—banks failing, the auto industry failing, massive layoffs across many sectors, and millions of people losing their homes—we gave our book another read. We realized that the lessons we share in this book—networking, selling, and negotiating, to name a few—are not only timeless, but more important than ever. Women in this "Great Recession" are keeping their jobs more than men, and record numbers of us are becoming the primary breadwinners for our families. As of July 2009, 1.4 million women lost their jobs versus 4.2 million men, mainly due to the decimation of the manufacturing and financial sectors. However, it's also important to note that women still only make 77 cents to every man's dollar; they are more affordable labor.

Faced with all of this bad news, we have two choices: we can let it overwhelm and depress us, or we can make the most of the fact that we're still out there working. We can work not just harder, but smarter and more efficiently, while growing our networks and maximizing our productivity. Rather then hunkering down and riding out the storm, we should seize opportunities—and believe us, opportunities are (still) out there—to continue to build a path to fulfillment and success. In this edition, we've added recession-friendly ideas and inspiration for doing just that. Girls, read this book and, to borrow a phrase from *Star Trek*, "Boldly go where no man has gone before."

PART ONE

make plans

one

you are here

Guess what? If you're not looking out for your career, then nobody is. If you want to be both passionate about what you do and successful, then you must take *control* of your professional destiny. Only you can determine who you are, what you can do, and where you want to go. This chapter will hold your hand while you step back and evaluate where you started, where you are on the career path today, how you got there, and most important, where you want to be tomorrow. We will ask you to ask yourself the tough questions: What does success mean for you? Are your fears holding you back? Is your job still working for you? Where did you envision yourself at this point? What kind of employee or manager are you? By diving deep into what motivates you professionally and reading the stories of women who have taken charge of their own careers, you will be armed with a better understanding of yourself and able to take that first step on the road to changing your life.

being the girl who makes it happen

We wrote this book for every woman out there who knows she can do more and wants to tackle the challenge. If you are stuck in your career, frustrated with your position within a company, or bored with the professional path you have chosen, then it is time to change your thinking. Start with a simple question: At the end of your life are you going to be proud of the extraordinary amount of time you have spent on this work?

If you've answered "yes," then use this book to get you to the next level by learning the skills to ask for what you deserve and confront your challenges head-on.

But if you've answered "no," then use this book to figure out what's missing—and what you need to do to take charge of your worklife. If you have gotten into the habit of writing a negative script for yourself, we'll work on the rewrite. Don't accept that you are the girl who *never gets what she wants*. Instead, become the girl who *makes it happen for herself*.

Think about this. According to a study done by the National Sleep Foundation, the average American spends forty-six hours per week at work. We'd bet it's actually higher than that, especially with inventions like the BlackBerry. And forty-six hours plus is a lot of time. Since the majority of our waking hours are spent working, we had better like what we're doing. The more we like what we do, the more energy we'll be able to devote to doing it well.

The key to finding happiness in what you do is in accepting who you are and what you want from your work life. Comparing your path to others' won't get you anywhere because your skills, values, personality, responsibilities, and even your location are all unique factors that will affect the trajectory of your career. If you're frustrated with where you are right now, then finding the answers to what you should do about it starts from looking within.

defining your own success

Over the last few years, we've asked hundreds of women to define success. For the women just starting out, success was most often a title above their peers, and the income to match. Many women in the middle of their careers felt successful if they had jobs that enabled them the flexibility they needed to be successful working mothers. And women late in their careers defined success as loving what they were doing professionally.

Wherever you are now, being aware of what success is to YOU will help motivate you to achieve the kind of career that is fulfilling and challenging and pays what you want, too. Being aware of your goal will also help you create the action plan.

Here are a few factors to consider when you're trying to define what success looks like.

- Is making big money a priority? If so, what are you willing to sacrifice for that money? If you sacrificed your personal life for money, would you still feel successful?
- Does size matter? Are you looking to manage a big team? Are you willing to train to become a strong leader? Do you have the confidence required to manage effectively, and if not, can you fake it?
- Is achieving a flexible schedule a factor in your success? If so, are you in a career that makes that possible?
- Does working part-time define success? Are you able to do that right now?
- Would you feel successful having a job that required you to travel?
- If you could just clock-in and clock-out with no residual stress, would that feel like success to you?
- Does it come down to being passionate about what you do professionally?

- Would you feel successful if you were working at a nonprofit?
- Do specific people in your industry inspire you, and if you worked with them, would you consider yourself successful?
- Is there a specific event that would define professional success for you? A great talk, producing a play, having a book published, receiving a glowing review or a reward?
- Is there an office that you have had your eye on, and if you were sitting in it, would you feel successful?
- If your team looked to you for guidance, support, and direction, would you feel successful?

Your personal definition of success will change during your lifetime, so check in from time to time to see how you are doing against your list. And feel free to change the list—priorities change as you mature. The key is to keep defining and redefining your success.

The sooner you can identify what values are important to you and to your dream career, the faster you can create the ideal work scenario. While answering the difficult questions posed in this chapter, go easy on yourself. Don't beat yourself up for not changing things sooner if you discover you are unhappy. Don't kick yourself for passing on a job offer that with the benefit of hindsight looks appealing. And don't self-limit by ruling out opportunities because you just don't think you are "that type of person."

For this book to work, you need to be honest and open to new ways of looking at your career and yourself.

FIVE CAREER-BOOSTING MANTRAS

As we speak to more women about their travels up, down, and off the ladder, we have heard several spiritual principles appearing in business advice. We love the idea of integrating these forms of wisdom because all of the people we find most professionally inspiring are at their essence spiritual people.

We have created this list of our five favorite career truths, mantras to say to yourself as you are getting ready to take control of your professional destiny and to recenter yourself when you feel off track.

Be Present Every Day in Your Life and in Your Work
Welcome New Ways of Thinking
Seek and Embrace Change
Act on Opportunities
Be Open to Meeting Your Next Mentor

how do you picture your career?

So you know you want things to change, but you're not exactly sure what you want the new picture to look like? Read through our list of statements and identify those that resonate:

- I want to stay where I am but would like to improve my situation with a raise and promotion.
- I want to stay with the company but am interested in moving into another area.
- I want to find another job in the same profession but with a different company.
- I want to break into another industry.
- I want to start my own business.

Keeping your career goal in mind will provide a focus while working through this book. But don't be surprised if by the last chapter you find yourself with an entirely new outlook on your professional future.

you yesterday

How did you even get here? Paying attention to where you've been can give you great insights into what you're doing now, whether it's right for you—or not.

Caitlin's favorite job was during college when she paid the rent by working at a bakery (if you ever find yourself in Amherst, Massachusetts, it's called The Black Sheep Deli). She loved the busy mornings when the shop was humming with students and professors grabbing cups of coffee and muffins before going to class. Because the bakery was in the center of town and campus, even when working she was in the loop on what was happening in the outside world. She loved taking lunch breaks with her coworkers, many of whom were in her classes at school, and she enjoyed being around the food. Most of all, she was thrilled to be working for someone who had his own thriving business, who created an environment that attracted customers and encouraged them to set up shop in the window seats to read books while drinking their afternoon lattes.

Did any of this indicate where she would end up? You tell us. Caitlin is now working in public relations (social, in-the-know), she writes books (feels like college), she specializes in food media, and she is the co-owner of two businesses.

While it's easy to identify what you don't like about your current situation, it isn't so easy to articulate what you do enjoy. You may find the answer by looking at your past.

Let's start digging. Take a piece of paper and write down the jobs you have held (paid and unpaid). Remembering how you spent your time at each one, choose the one where you were happiest. Write down the reasons for your satisfaction. Was it teamwork? Was it the corporate culture? Was it your boss who made it your favorite? Was it how you spent your day? The clients you dealt with? The skills and lessons learned? Now look at your list. These are the qualities you want to add into your current work situation.

Now, to help save yourself the pain and agony of looking at professions that won't energize you or make you happy, identify your least favorite job. What were the reasons for your discontent? Were you micromanaged? Underappreciated? Uninspired? Was it a negative place to spend your day? Hopefully these are workplace qualities that you can avoid!

For those of you who think that your personal and professional lives are entirely separate entities, look closer at your Career Timeline and remember what was happening at home when you held each job. You may notice that during a particularly trying time in your personal life your career stalled. After a much-needed vacation you returned to work with an updated résumé and energy to start looking for something better. While focusing on taking charge of your career, don't forget to take charge of your personal life, too. When things are in balance it is significantly easier to think clearly and make small or large changes.

Last, look at where you started and where you are right now. Did you have a plan or did things just happen? Have you had a vision for your career and made decisions all along moving you toward your goal? Or does it feel like you have always sat in the passenger seat as your career drove itself along?

Jen Ramos, the promotional director of Vroman's Bookstore in

California, had no plan for her career but found her path through her jobs.

> When I got out of high school I wasn't sure what exactly I wanted to be when I grew up. I went to junior college for a couple of years and still couldn't figure it out. It wasn't until I went out into the work force that I was able to find my way.

But it was a side job that pointed her in the right direction.

> In my early twenties I worked in an accounting department of a major corporation, but on the side I managed a friend's band. I loved their music and wanted as many people as I could find to hear them. So I took on the job of promoting them. I booked shows, I submitted their music to radio, and I eventually landed them their first record contract, along with their first record producer. While I was working with the band I found that I needed to be in a real job that would help me with contacts and resources to help them—and that led me to my next favorite job, working for an independent record company. I loved the promotions part of the job. Succeeding in getting the band on the radio or seeing large crowds at their shows was the cherry on top. I eventually left the record company, but I always stayed in promotions. Today, I am a promotional director for a wonderful independent bookstore.

you today

So you know where you came from and what you have done. What about the here and now? Does the job you have still work for you? Do you still work for it? This section of the chapter will help you take that long necessary look at work life as you know it.

DOES YOUR CURRENT JOB STILL FIT?

As two people who have been publicists, event planners, marketing consultants, television producers, and authors, we're living proof that there is nothing wrong with changing your career midcourse or even more. Take an honest look at what you are doing right now to earn a living and be prepared for the fact that you may have outgrown it. Even though you went to school for law, you may have developed a passion for screenwriting or an interest in travel and want to make a change. You may have taken your current job because the salary was just too high to walk away from but have found yourself hating it. You may have signed up for a Web designing class in your spare time and discovered that not only did you love it but you are great at it. You may really enjoy what you do, but because of family responsibilities you need to make more money doing it.

Did you take the job just for the money?

If so, ask yourself if the money is still worth your valuable time. If not, then that is good to know because instead of trying to create a better scenario where you are, maybe you should be focusing on moving to another company or starting a new profession.

Does your job challenge you?

This may not be a priority for you. Sometimes we go through phases in our lives where our personal life is too draining to crave challenges at work. Or, you may have outside interests that require focus and energy and you don't have much else to give. But, if it is important for you to be challenged every day, then that is something that your job has to offer.

Do your skills still apply?

Especially in the technology industry, you are constantly updating your skill-set to adapt to new systems and information. If everything around you and in your field is speeding by you and you don't have the interest or energy to keep up, then your job no longer fits. On the flip side, perhaps you have developed skills that surpass the opportunities offered at your job and you could have a better situation elsewhere.

Does it still pay enough?

We aren't asking you if your job is paying you what you want (that comes later), but as your personal responsibilities—children, home-ownership, even dogs cost money—change you may not be making enough.

Do you still like living where you need to in order to keep this job?

There could be a million reasons you would rather live somewhere else, but if those reasons are becoming impossible to ignore, then you need to seriously weigh that against staying put for this job.

Have your family's needs changed?

It could be that suddenly you find yourself responsible for an aging parent, or your children need you to be home more than you are, or your partner has a job opportunity that will require more travel, leaving much of the running of the home on your shoulders. Whatever it may be, there could come a day when, because of your changing personal responsibilities, your job no longer works.

Are you still passionate about what you do?

There may come a day when you realize that you aren't. Don't ignore that "lightbulb" moment. Alicia Rockmore, cofounder of Buttoned Up, Inc., a "company dedicated to helping busy women tame the chaos in their lives," as she puts it, shared this with us: "After a successful fourteen years in packaged goods, I remember one day, saying good-bye to my two-year-old daughter, getting in the car to drive to work and just realizing that I was tired of trying to sell stuff that people really didn't need more of. No one really needs to eat one more cup of mayo than they did the year before. No one really needs to buy more packaged rice to serve their families. It just seemed ridiculous and that is when I knew I needed to start something on my own."

If your job is no longer satisfying, then don't gloss over that essential truth but ask yourself why that may be. Is it the job, the pay, the town or city you live in? Revisit the goals stated earlier in this chapter. Do you need to think about changing professions or going back to school?

examining career boredom

Sometimes we find ourselves in jobs that are comfortable and familiar and mind-numbingly boring. A few of us find ourselves in careers that we are good at but that are not necessarily good for us. If you are just going through the motions and floating through the day unengaged, uninspired, and unmotivated, it is time to shake things up.

Now, if you are in the lucky position of liking your industry but are bored with your job, it is time for some informational and informal interviews with people in your network. When we were in publishing, we had a woman in our company come to us for an interview. She was in sales and we were in publicity, and she wanted to know everything about our side of things. She asked all the right questions, including how we spent the majority of our day, what we liked and didn't like about it, was there room for growth beyond the vice presidential level? She told us that she was setting up similar meetings with contacts in marketing and editorial so she could get a broad understanding of publishing. She told us she loved the business of books but that she knew that being in sales was not for her. If you are still enthused by your industry, don't throw in the towel yet and consider yourself lucky that you found yourself in a career that might be perfect for you with a little tweaking.

If you are uninspired by both the daily responsibilities and the bigger picture then it is likely time for a change. Ellen Malloy, founder of Paperclip, Inc., recommends jumping ship if you're miserable, "When I am really bored, frustrated or otherwise in a funk for a long while, I move on. I guess I don't see the point of forcing myself into a job or profession I don't like. If I did, I probably wouldn't go far because I am probably not going to be great at the job and I won't be happy along the way. Work isn't life, but it is certainly a place where you spend a majority of your waking hours. You need to be happy there."

changes that may change your thinking about your job

There are a number of common changes that can inspire you to rethink your future at your company, but we encourage you to give yourself time to adjust before making any rash decisions when you face one of these situations.

- A New Boss
- Change in Company Policy
- Department Reconfiguration
- A Corporate Merger
- Layoffs
- Rapid Expansion

- Change in Responsibilities
- New Hires

5 REASONS TO EMBRACE SUCCESS

1. It will make you a happier person.
2. You will inspire those around you.
3. Without limits you are limitless.
4. You deserve to feel successful.
5. It keeps you growing and changing.

FACTS ABOUT WOMEN AND SUCCESS

Catalyst (www.catalystwomen.org), a leading research and advisory organization that works to help women in business, did this survey on success strategies for women.

How women succeeded:
- Consistently exceeding expectations (69 percent)
- Successfully managing others (49 percent)
- Developing a style with which male managers are comfortable (47 percent)
- Having a recognized expertise in a specific content area (46 percent)

What holds women back from top management?
Women executives say:
- Lack of significant general management/line experience (47 percent)
- Exclusion from informal networks of communication (41 percent)

what do you really bring to the table?

Many of us play the blame game instead of taking responsibility for our shortcomings. Hanging responsibility for your small salary and insignificant title on your boss will get you nowhere. Complaining to others about your "boring" job won't get you any closer to an exciting one. Taking charge of your destiny will start only when you get real with yourself about your professional strengths and weaknesses. If you have a hard time looking in the mirror and assessing your weaknesses, run them by the women in your circle of friends. Financial adviser Tara Prindible went to women in her network when she was having problems with her career. "The hardest part for me has been humbling myself and becoming comfortable with telling my sphere of influence that I am not happy where I am, but that I have a vision of where I want to be. These women have been a tremendous sounding board for me, and have given me honest feedback about what they see as good qualities in me, and also what has some room for improvement."

Here is a wide range of questions that will start you thinking about your contributions and attitude objectively. Knowing your strengths, weaknesses, and point of view will help you as you begin making decisions about next steps. Take a deep breath, promise to answer every single question honestly, and when stuck ask someone who knows you well professionally to give you feedback:

At work do you:
- Contribute to meetings;
- Proactively seek more responsibility; and
- Challenge yourself by taking on difficult projects?

If you answered "yes," then congratulations—you are a girl taking charge. If you answered "no," then you came to the right place.

As a manager do you:
- Share the big picture with your team;
- Give clear direction;
- Mentor someone on your staff;
- Offer constructive criticism; and
- Make yourself available to your reports?

If you answered "yes," then congratulations—you are a good manager. If you answered "no," then you will soon see why getting the best out of your employees is the road to success.

As an employee are you:
- Committing yourself to the organization;
- Walking away from water cooler griping;
- Proactively seeking more responsibility;
- Looking to learn something new;
- Challenging yourself by taking on difficult projects;
- Respecting your leadership and company at large; and
- Content with what you do each day?

If you answered "yes," then please come and work for us! If you answered "no," then you might want to start thinking about big changes.

As a coworker do you:

· Share credit;
· Respect the ideas of others;
· Contribute ideas and solutions;
· Offer to assist others with projects whenever possible; and
· Mentor someone?

If you answered "yes," it sounds like you are great to work with. If you answered "no," then you need to know that creating a real team among your coworkers will make you both happier and more successful.

As a member of your industry are you:

· Passionate about it; and
· Thrilled to be a part of it?

The only answer here that will really work in the long run is "yes," because life is too short to be a part of something that doesn't turn you on. If you aren't passionate about your job or your industry in general, then you can only get so far.

how do you work best today?

To either kick butt at your current job or to help clarify a new direction for yourself, spend a few minutes pinpointing under what circumstances you work best. The structure of your job itself—the workday, staffing, the style of the managers above you, the stress level—contributes more than you might realize to your happiness and productivity.

At what time of day do you work best?

Sure, everyone talks about the first thing in the morning being the best time for productivity and the mid-afternoon the worst, but that doesn't hold true for everyone. Caitlin's husband actually spends several hours each week working at 2:00 A.M. because he finds that he is more focused at that time. We can't imagine it, but it seems to work for him.

Are you motivated by stress and pressure or debilitated by them?

If you are in a high-stress field, then that better energize you or you are going to end up depleted and burned out. If you buckle under pressure, then that is a good thing to know about yourself, and if you have not already, focus on a profession that isn't structured by deadlines, emergencies, crises, and tension.

Does lots of money mean lots of good work?

If you are the type of person that needs to be paid really well before you can deliver your best work, then you must take that into consideration before making any career changes. Switching professions means that you most likely won't be taking your high salary with you, so if that is going to be an issue, then you might want to think twice about starting something new.

Do you need to be managed or do you work better when you are autonomous?

We had an employee who worked best when we were managing her very closely. Unfortunately for all of us, this realization came almost too late. For months she felt neglected and we felt that she wasn't delivering. If she had known herself well enough to ask for more guidance and if we had been more clued in to what motivated her, then all would have been spared a lot of grief.

Do you work best with support staff below you?

Some of us find assistants more hindrance than help, but others can't work well without someone to delegate work. It is essential to know where you fall because it will help you staff yourself in the best way possible or find well-staffed companies.

you tomorrow

Before making any changes in the direction of your career, it is important to take a long hard look at yourself. Hopefully, after reading this chapter and spending a little time reflecting on your work history, your skills and the attitude you bring to the table, you are in a position to look forward. You know if the job you are in right now is satisfying, what situation you need in order to work best, and have thought about how you pictured your career. You are now ready to begin taking the steps to find true happiness and success at work.

girl taking charge

JESS MILLS, PRINCIPAL AND DIRECTOR OF MARKETING AND INVESTOR RELATIONS AT A MAJOR NATIONAL HEDGE FUND

As two people who have one heck of a time wrapping our heads around hedge funds, bonds, and basically anything having to do with Wall Street, we were so impressed with Jess's dedication to her career. She had some great advice to share with us on managing your career.

Did you know what you wanted to be when you grew up?
When I was a kid, I knew I either wanted to be a veterinarian or run a business. Not sure what I based this on, come to think of it.

But I ended up in economics. When I started my first job in finance after college, I told my first boss that I wanted to "manage people." As you can imagine he laughed. I was twenty-two years old and I had zero experience in finance. Fast forward ten years, I became a partner at the second financial firm I worked for. You can't underestimate the payoff for dedication, hard work—and commitment to the business in which you work. I really only have had three jobs in this field and my loyalty was always rewarded.

Have you always had a plan for your career?
It's been pretty organic. I thought I was going to be an economist when I got out of college—and then spent a year in Washington, D.C., doing economic and environmental consulting. A year into it we closed a multibillion-dollar business transaction for the Department of Energy. When I saw the economics on the deal, I realized that I was sitting on the wrong side of the table and that realization got me to New York and into finance.

What keeps you motivated to move forward in your career?
Doing something I love, working with people I respect, and having fun . . . and always growing.

Why do you think you have done well in your career?
Positive thinking is critical to success. People will rally around the person who is positive and confident. I don't mean that you have to be some drippy sap; I mean that you can face a tough situation and see that embedded in the issue is something to laugh about and a positive direction to move toward.

In your opinion, what do women need to do in order to be successful in their careers?
Realize there are rules to every game—and men make a lot of them. Watch, listen, and learn. Every business has a formula for success. Watch successful people around you and try to take the best tools they use and bring them into your world. Also remember that you are not everyone's "mommy" in the office . . . nor are you going to succeed by sleeping with anyone. On the flip side, a

woman's level of emotional understanding offers us an ability to build different and often stronger relationships. And there is a lot to be gained from those relationships. Be professional. Dress professionally, behave professionally, but still bring your personality into the mix. Be proactive, work hard, and be humble. Cherish your successes but, more important, own your failures and learn from them.

Do you have any advice for women feeling in a professional rut?
Take a step back and figure out why you are in the rut in the first place. Is it something personal or is it structural? Don't like your colleagues? Does someone else you work with have a job you think is appealing? Sit down with your boss and talk about goals and expectations. In so many ways, if you communicate your goals, your boss will help you to get there.

What are some steps women should take if they want to move up the ladder?
Work hard and be loyal to the people who can help you take it to the next level and to those who can take that opportunity away. Don't gossip and don't give anyone an opportunity to cut you down. Being kindhearted will help you—you don't have to be a ruthless bitch to succeed—even in finance!

a view from the ladder

Andrea Farnum, coprincipal of Full Bloom, an events company, television personality, and columnist, was a New York City police officer before immersing herself in the culinary business. She started her four-year career in law enforcement in a patrol car and ended up in narcotics as an undercover agent. We spoke to her about the decision to join the force, what it was like working in a male-dominated profession, and what ultimately spurred her to make a change.

Can you share with us your interest in becoming a police officer?

I never had any desire to be a cop. I went to school for journalism and after college was working in Manhattan as an editorial assistant making $11,000 a year. Years earlier my uncle, who was a cop, signed up all the nieces and nephews for the police department entrance exam. I took the written test and scored very high. It can sometimes take years to get on the police force, so frankly I looked at the exam as a sociological experiment. I never thought about passing, never mind how scoring so high would impact my future. But there I was sitting at my desk, making a pittance, and I get a call that there is an opening in the next police academy class. Starting salary was . . . $30,000! It didn't take long for me to do the math. As bizarre as it sounds, I did it for the money.

But you stayed?

I ended up staying for four years. After the six months of basically boot camp, I wanted to see what it was like on the street. I worked in a patrol car and had a partner for a year and a half until I applied for a position as an undercover narcotics officer and was accepted.

Did you feel you were going to hit a glass ceiling as a woman in the New York Police Department?

The good thing about the NYPD is that most promotions are done by tests, which pretty much evens the playing field. But it was a strange experience to be in such a male-dominated field. I really did get an education in the male sex and their nuances. Clearly, in order to get along, I had to be "one of the boys." But I was adamant that they were not going to make a man out of me!

So why leave the force?

I married a cop from my precinct and decided it was time for a change. I had always had an interest in antiques and was an avid collector, so when I saw a classified ad for an assistant to a high-end dealer, I applied. I worked in that business in one form or another for four years.

But you ended up in the food business?

After deciding that the antiques business wasn't creative enough, I began cooking for small house parties on the side. One thing led to another and it blossomed into a full-time business.

Do you have any advice for people who are unhappy in their current professions?

I really don't think there is an exact formula for happiness. Obviously, we have to take care of our financial obligations before blindly making changes. However, I am a big proponent of following your gut. If you have a passion or love for something and would like to pursue it as a career—you need to do it! You can start it part-time if you are too skittish, but you need to just do it. Life is too short and we live too long now to be stuck doing soul-numbing work.

Anything you would like to say to women who are stuck and don't have a plan for their career?

Know yourself. If you don't know yourself, then work on it. Go to therapy, write in a journal, meditate, go to church, whatever works for you. Once you are in touch with yourself, you are less likely to get in your own way.

getting where you want to go

You've figured out where you are. And realized you're not satisfied. Of course, you're not. Ambitious girls never are. Ambitious girls want to know where they are going. We got this job. Now, what's the next job? We got a raise. When's the next one coming? If you're a star performer (or on the path to being a star performer), then making a plan for your career is the next step. It won't be set in stone, because life happens, and opportunities come up and circumstances change, but it's really helpful to consider your options and visualize an ideal path for yourself.

We didn't do this enough early in our careers. And since we didn't know what we wanted, we focused on the negative. "We don't want to work for that woman." "We don't want to be making lunch reservations for the rest of our lives." "We can't live on this salary for one more day." Of course these are exactly the issues you should be thinking about: who do you want to work with; what kind of work do you want to be doing; how much do you need to earn? But we weren't planning; we were reacting, and usually out of frustration.

You can do better. Creating a plan for your work life (even if it's just a list of ideas about who you are and where you want to be) is worth the effort, and this chapter will show you how to get it done. We'll also throw in some much-needed information on résumé-writing and skill-building because these are both important tools to help you take control of your career.

the career plan

To begin the process, you're going to have to free yourself from all career barriers: lack of motivation, apathy, procrastination, family pressure—including expectations to work in the family business, follow a certain career path, or avoid careers that are below your status—and peer pressure, among others. Career planning is an evolving process, so take it slowly and easily. Think in terms of short-term and long-term goals. Short-term goals are up to five years: they're the steps you need to take to make your long-term goals possible. Long-term goals are just that, a look down the road. Where do you want to be in ten or fifteen years?

Until recently we didn't bother with long-term goals. We could barely get a handle on today; who needs to focus ten years down the road? But when we started writing the Girl's Guide books, our time-lines automatically got longer. Books take years to write, so when we started looking at the five books that we wanted to write, all of sudden we had a ten-year plan!

Let's start with short-term planning, because when done right it delivers immediate results. And who doesn't love instant gratification?

what am i doing today, tomorrow, and next year?

Successful short-term career planning involves developing specific, realistic goals and objectives. The easiest place to begin is by looking around and above you. What do the other jobs look like in your organization? What skills do the people in those roles possess that you don't? How do you find out? Begin with a thorough self-evaluation in the following categories:

SKILLS

Do you have all of the skills necessary to achieve your new career goals? Are there skills that you could acquire that would make you more hirable as well as secure a better salary? Are there new skills that you want to develop before taking any next steps with your career?

PERSONALITY

Do you know what motivates you? What you need at work to be happy? What is your overall attitude about yourself and work? How do you work best? Do you thrive when working with a team or are you a more independent worker? Try taking a personality test to help you answer this; there's a free personality test online at www.ustechnicaljobs.com.

INTERESTS

What are your hobbies? What physical activities do you like to do? What clubs do you belong to? Are you social? It is helpful to see if there are clues in your personal life and interests that could offer career direction or networking opportunities.

VALUES

What are you looking for your job to give you? Financial security? Flexibility? Travel? Fame and prestige? You should take your values into account when making any decision about your career.

If you're really honest, self-evaluation will generate as many questions as answers. When Kim realized that her inability to manage her time was holding her back from a promotion, she started reading time-management books and mimicking other people's systems until she found one that worked for her.

Now is the time to crack the books or hop online. Keep the following categories in mind:

EDUCATION

What do you need to learn to move forward in your career or find a new job with a higher salary? Would you need an advanced degree, or are there individual classes that would help you? Doing research can help you determine exactly where you should be applying yourself and what skills and training employers in your chosen field are looking for.

MONEY

You could be looking at things such as your worth in the marketplace at your current level; the salaries offered in industries you are interested in; the cost of living in other areas if you want to relocate; what an ideal raise would look like; your retirement goals; or the cost of child care if you are planning a family.

A NEW JOB

Are there other jobs at your company that you are interested in learning more about? What does the hiring landscape look like in your industry these days? Is your résumé or bio up to date? Are you networking enough and staying connected to the people you meet? Do you read trade publications to see if job opportunities are listed? Is there a headhunter that you have heard good things about?

A NEW PROFESSION

What industry do you want to break into? What are the options for getting a foot in the door? Do you know anyone in that profession who can give you advice? Are there trade magazines or newspapers that you should be reading to give you an idea of what is going on? What kind of education and skills do you need to succeed in this profession? Can you get a job moonlighting to get practical experience?

RELOCATING

Where do you want to live? What does the job situation look like there? Are housing costs reasonable? Is your family onboard? What about the school and child care options? Subscribe to the local paper so you have a better idea of what the place offers. Reach out to local job hunters and realtors to start researching on your behalf.

take action

At this point, you should have created a list of objectives that you want to accomplish in the next three to five years. You have done all the research and know what you need to do. Time to take action—in the form of an action plan.

An action plan is a simple list of all of the tasks that you need to carry out to achieve your objective. It differs from a simple "to-do list" because it is focused on one goal exclusively. For example, if your goal is to get a new job with one of your competitors, your action plan would include steps such as updating your résumé, evaluating your network to see if anyone can help you secure an interview, and researching the new company. Write the tasks in the order you need to complete them so that you have a running status report of your progress.

You don't have to make action plans for each objective right away. Prioritize your objectives and then make action plans for them as you go along. One of our toughest bosses gave us some great advice that we'll pass along: always do the hardest thing first. It makes the rest of the day, week, or project seem easy. This process can be overwhelming, so focus on one objective at a time. And don't forget to give yourself credit for taking these steps to move your career plan forward.

you on paper: the résumé

Updating the résumé is a tough task. After years of not having or needing one, we wrote one as research for this book and it was torture. How do you sum up the accomplishments of a career (even if it's only two years old) on one piece of paper? How do you distinguish yourself among the thousands of graduates who are applying for a position they saw advertised on www.monster.com? Your résumé must sell your accomplishments and talents. Current research shows that only one interview is granted for every two-hundred résumés received by the average employer. And the average employer spends about twenty seconds scanning it. Twenty seconds. Every single word needs to make an impact. The top half of the first page needs to be succinct and sexy. You're not telling your life story—you're selling yourself. Think advertising copy but stay true to the facts. Research the industry standard for each position and make sure you follow it. When our editor's husband was transitioning from being a book editor to the consulting field, his advisers were adamant that he not state an "objective" on his résumé. It's a big no-no in that field, and had he included an "objective," it would have sent a red flag to the hiring manager that this candidate hadn't done his due diligence on the industry and severely handicapped his chances of getting an interview.

Once you've established the industry standard, target your résumé for each specific job—modify (or remove) your objective and move accomplishments higher or lower based on the job requirements. Carefully read the job listing and make sure that the qualities and skills you are selling are the ones the employer is buying.

Even if you aren't looking for a new job right now, it's important to always have a current résumé, just in case. You never know when a golden opportunity will leave a message on your voice mail! And getting your résumé into shape is a terrific way to really think about your accomplishments.

Every résumé should include your contact information, objective, summary of qualifications, skills and accomplishments, relevant work history, education, and personal interests. When writing your résumé, it's easiest to work backward—begin with the easy stuff, your work history and education, and then flesh out your skills and accomplishments. Review those skills and accomplishments and choose the best ones to highlight in the summary. Finally, after reviewing a specific job advertisement to which you're applying, target your objective accordingly.

Looks count. Print your résumé on heavy white or off-white paper. Choose a consistent font and style. Plenty of samples are available online to mimic. Proofread it and proofread it again—and ask someone else to take a look, too. Hiring managers have zero tolerance for sloppy résumés. Tossing sloppy offerings is the fastest way to trim down the huge pile. Remember, they are scanning for twenty seconds!

To write your "objective" you must consider what qualities would set a truly exceptional candidate apart from a merely good one. Your objective should demonstrate that you are the ideal candidate for the specific position. For example, an objective from a publicist candidate that would make an impression on us would look like this:

objective

A publicist position in an organization where strong media relations skills, contacts, and a results-oriented approach are needed.

The "Summary" or "Summary of Qualifications" consists of several concise statements that focus the reader's attention on the most important qualities, achievements, and abilities you have to offer. It's also the place to include professional characteristics (extremely enthusiastic, a natural media booker, great people skills, etc.).

Every word must count. If you're responding to a monster.com ad or another online service, remember that hiring managers search for key words, so make sure your summary section includes as many keywords as possible. According to monster.com, "Keywords are the backbone for résumé scanning technology. If a company is seeking a chief financial officer, it may do a keyword search through thousands of résumés to find candidates with experience in tax, treasury, cash management, currency hedging, and foreign exchange. If you don't have those words in your résumé, you will be passed over."

The "Skills and Accomplishments" section follows the summary and goes into more detail about each of your skills. Share your successes, what happened as a result of your efforts, and highlight your talents.

List your relevant work experience, education, and a few personal interests. If you don't have much work experience, then make sure you highlight the skills and values you've learned in school, internships, and nonrelevant work experience.

A sample résumé for the new girl in the workforce (and we hired this one!):

NAME
Address
Phone
E-mail

OBJECTIVE
An assistant position in a public relations agency that needs an organized, fast learner who wants to learn public relations.

SUMMARY
Highly motivated recent graduate with knowledge of media buying, conflict resolution, marketing plans, office organization, administrative skills, and fluent in Spanish.

SKILLS AND ACCOMPLISHMENTS
- Mastered skills needed to be promoted in six months to media-buying position
- Generated new ideas in youth marketing at quarterly sales meeting
- Was go-to contact for client problems
- Worked to deadline each day
- Worked effectively on teams
- Proficient in all Windows versions, Microsoft Office: Access, Excel, FrontPage, PowerPoint, Word, MS-DOS, Adobe Photoshop, Premiere and other versions, Goldmine, Macintosh, and IBM operating systems
- Type 45wpm
- Fluent in speaking, reading, and writing Spanish

WORK EXPERIENCE

ALLOY MEDIA + MARKETING, NEW YORK, NY

Media Buyer, February 2006–Present
- Service larger accounts in conjunction with outside salesperson, provide rates to clients in Customized Advertising Reports for review and accurate newspaper placement
- Liaison with clients, sales team, and publications, manage day-to-day sales transactions of client
- Generate insertion orders, send ad material, and confirm status of campaign
- Resolve placement issues such as incorrect material, missed run dates, and headline changes
- Maintain efficient and extensive filing systems for easy retrieval of information electronically as well as hard files
- Attend quarterly sales on-site training meetings and discuss new opportunities in youth marketing

Media Assistant, August 2005–February 2006
- Purchased newspaper advertising space
- Generated insertion orders, mailed out graphics to publications, confirmed ad space and receipt of material
- Resolved placement issues such as incorrect material, missed run dates, and headline changes
- Worked effectively in a team environment, managed all accounts assigned by team manager
- Assisted team members with their accounts and participated in monthly team meetings

ANNA SUI CORPORATION, NEW YORK, NY

Intern, January 2003–March 2003
- Provided administrative support to showroom/sales department. Duties included but were not limited to placing orders, tracking samples, answering phones, filing, faxing, and scheduling
- Assisted in selling fall 2003 line to prominent department store buyers

EDUCATION
Skidmore College, Saratoga Springs, NY
Bachelor of Arts, Graduated: 2005
Major in Foreign Languages and Arts, minor in Management and Business

References Available Upon Request

A sample résumé for a senior position looks like this:

NAME

Address, Phone, E-mail

Objective To secure a senior health care communications position in an organization where creativity, staff development, and strategic thinking toward cause-related and drug marketing efforts are needed.

Summmary Skills and Accomplishments

I am a member of the senior management team at an award-winning specialist international health care PR agency. As such, I share responsibility for the overall direction and profitability of the agency. In addition, I hold specific responsibilities for staff development, management, and training. Although I work on a variety of ethical and OTC accounts covering all stages of the product life cycle, I am also the agency lead for a very high profile company, managing a team of eight people and a budget in excess of $1 million. My work on this business has resulted in significant achievements for the Drug brand in terms of sales and reputation, and for the client, and for our staff both personally and professionally. Having already received a variety of prizes for our work from several specialist industry panels, we were most recently awarded the prestigious SABRE Award for Best Cause-Related Marketing for our work in developing and implementing the first ever global breast cancer awareness campaign.

The qualities that I believe I have been allowed to foster and develop at Company are those of which I am most proud and intend to bring with me to any work environment. They include a keen sense of responsibility for the business and its people; a desire to be the best; and the drive to create passion for my job and the work we do on a daily basis. As a senior professional in the business, I have also worked hard to hone my interpersonal skills—always searching to combine a youthful sense of fun with perspective, maturity, and responsibility.

Other experience: 1990–1994

- Consultant and Research Assistant for HIV Education Prevention Project, New York
- Education & Literacy Assistant, WNET/TV, New York
- Production Assistant, *The Geraldo Rivera Show*, New York
- Volunteer Supervisor, City Councilman Campaign, New York
- Intern Assistant to Vice Chair, Democratic National Committee, Washington, D.C.

Education, Awards, and Honors:

05/06	SABRE Award, Short-listed, Best Public Awareness Campaign (winners to be announced in May 2006); Global launch of IBIS II (breast cancer prevention study)
09/05	Award Winner, Best PR Campaign, Redefining Hope & Beauty
06/05	SABRE Award, Best Cause-Related Campaign, Redefining Hope & Beauty, AstraZeneca
03/05	Giant Award for Creativity—Redefining Hope & Beauty, AstraZeneca
03/05	MOSCAR Awards, Best Media Campaign and Best Patient Advocacy Campaign
12/04	Employee of the Year
06/04	Communiqué Award, Best Product Campaign
05/04	NLP Master Practitioner Certificate, International Teaching Seminars, London
08/01 & 02	Awards for Client Development and Best Client Work
06/93	National Association of Hispanic Journalists Scholarship Recipient
05/90	College, MA, USA: BA in Political Science and Latin American Studies
05/90	College, MA, USA: Sigma Iota Rho (National Honors Society for International Relations)
05/90	College, MA, USA: Student Government Achievement Award

Interests:

Professional and personal coaching, acting, volunteer work, and handbags!

References available upon request.

a short look down the long road

If short-term planning focuses on the attainable objectives, then long-term planning focuses on the attainable skills that you should acquire to be successful in your chosen profession with a little futurist activity thrown in.

According to one of our favorite career sites, www.quintcareers .com, "Core workplace skills include: communications (verbal and written), critical and creative thinking, teamwork and team-building, listening, social, problem-solving, decision-making, interpersonal, project management, planning and organizing, computer/technology, and commitment to continuous/lifelong learning."

Futurist activity is really trend-watching. Futurists know what's going to happen before it does—a nice skill if you can get it. The fact is that in the fast-changing world in which we work, it is hard enough keeping up, no less staying one step ahead. However, information about the future of your industry will always help you adjust your skills accordingly. Information about where things are going could encourage you to learn a new skill that will help down the road—whether in the form of a promotion, a job change, or even a new industry.

DO YOU HAVE WHAT IT TAKES TO BE AN ENTREPRENEUR?

If your arms are starting to get tired climbing up the corporate ladder, your ticket to success may not be another résumé drop. You may just want to start your own business. Although it seems like a dream scenario—working from home, being your own boss, taking a day off just because you can—the reality of being a small business owner is not quite so sunny and is full of its own special challenges. Be sure to ask yourself these key questions before you make that big jump!

Are you willing to work hard?

You better be. If you decide to open your own business, you will be working your butt off, and your hours will be well beyond 9–5/Monday–Friday. If you have always wanted to be an entrepreneur, know that you can't do it at half-speed.

Can you live on an income that may ebb and flow?

The first year will most likely be a financial roller coaster, and the second one may be as well, so you need to have a handle on your personal and professional funds. As the co-owners of a public relations firm, we have had our share of very bad and very good years.

Do you enjoy learning?

If you are naturally curious about how things work and enjoy developing new skills, then chances are you will embrace the many opportunities for learning that present themselves. As a business owner you will learn everything from how to work with a designer on your company logo and what taxes to file to how to sell yourself and manage a staff.

Are you open to suggestions and help from outside?

Chances are pretty good that you don't know how to do everything, and since running a business requires a wide range of skills and expertise, you will need to ask for help. We are excellent publicists, but when we wanted to create www.girlsguidetobusiness.com, we had to ask for help.

Are you confident or can you fake it?

As an entrepreneur you will need to sell yourself, your company, your products, or your services to potential customers. If you are insecure (and we all are in some way or another, so don't feel bad about it) and just can't pretend otherwise, then you may want to consider taking on a partner who excels at this.

The upsides of owning your own business are immeasurable, but first and foremost you have more control over your professional destiny when you are your own boss, so we encourage everyone to at least consider it. If it looks like that's what you want to do and you want more information on next steps, pick up our first book, *The Girl's Guide to Starting Your Own Business*.

girl taking charge

As a life coach Jennifer Lee of Change Journey Coaching has helped hundreds of women find satisfaction and happiness in their careers and lives.

Why do you think that women in particular have such a hard time thinking big when it comes to their careers?
As women, we're often so busy helping others that we're not helping ourselves. We also tend to avoid conflict, believing that to move up the ladder means playing hardball, and that's not necessarily a game we want to play. Plus, with female leaders still sorely underrepresented in top executive ranks, it can be tough for us to find great role models—especially ones who successfully balance the many roles of career woman, mother, wife, friend, and so on.

All that aside, I believe that we have an important opportunity to start claiming our true worth in the workplace (and in the world!). Emotional intelligence gives us lovely ladies a leg up when it comes to relationship building and influence. By valuing our innate strengths of connection, nurturing, intuition, and empathy, we can reinvent what our impact and contribution is in our work.

How do you know when it's time to make a big professional change?
The most important thing is to get really clear on what it is you want. Write it down, visualize it, and believe you will make it hap-

pen. Set two or three goals to help keep you on track and identify people to help you and to hold you accountable. And know that a significant change like this doesn't happen overnight. You should break your transition down into baby steps. Here are some ideas to get you going:

- Research your new profession. Surf the Web, read trade journals and books, join networking associations.
- Find allies and lean into your support network. Let encouraging friends know how they can specifically assist you.
- Talk to people you admire. Ask them what they did to get where they are.
- Take a class. If you're interested in running a vineyard someday, take a weekend course on wine tasting or viticulture.
- Volunteer in a role or field you're interested in. If you want to move from IT to marketing, see if you can volunteer at a nonprofit to create their marketing strategy.
- Moonlight or do some pro bono consulting on the side. This will give you some great experience in your new line of work in a low-risk way.
- Seek out opportunities in your current job to gain exposure to new areas or skills that you're interested in.
- Find ways to meet your needs in a personal way. If you're craving more creativity on the job, think about how you can bring more creativity into your free time. Sometimes simply allowing space for what we want enables us to attract more of it into other areas of our lives.
- Also, don't forget to practice self care! Changing your career is no small feat, so remember to do nice things for yourself along the way.

When you're ready to make the leap, it's important to let go of your old world in order to fully step into the new. Do what you need to in order to say good-bye to your previous "identity," routine, and lifestyle. Remember to honor what gifts they provided you for the next phase of your career. And please, celebrate!!! Have a launch party and invite all the wonderful people who supported you in your journey.

Do you have any other tips or advice for women picking up this book and willing to take the time to evaluate their professional dreams?

Sometimes the clues to your dream job are right under your nose. So, look around you and see what stands out. What type of books do you enjoy reading? How do you like to spend your time and money? What do you love to talk about with your friends and family?

Gain a fresh perspective by trying something totally new. Pick up a magazine that you've never read before on something you know absolutely nothing about. Strike up a conversation with a complete stranger. Take a different route to work. The point is to shake up your normal routine and be open to what sparks your interest.

Invent your "dream job" job description. Include the title, salary, responsibilities, required skills and experience, location, hours, and anything else you desire. If you're a visual gal, make a "dream job" collage. Then imagine that you are applying for this "dream job" and that, of course, you are the perfect fit. Craft a cover letter that extols your strengths, passions, qualifications, and key accomplishments (even if you're just making it up at this point). Don't worry, you won't be showing it to anyone. This is purely for your own inspiration, so get creative and think big! When you write it down, you can make it happen. You can also enlist experienced support. Work with a life coach to uncover your passions, values, and life vision. Partner with a career counselor to identify your aptitudes, skills, and talents. You don't have to go it alone!

a view from the ladder

Lisa is a vice president of program distribution for a major television production company responsible for many hit shows. She graduated from the University of Pennsylvania with a communications degree and a minor in Italian studies in 1990. Lisa had two passions back then (now too, actually): jewelry design and documentary film.

She moved to New York after she graduated to pursue a career in jewelry design that lasted about one week when she realized that she'd never be able to pay her rent on what she earned (although she did turn it into a fulfilling weekend apprenticeship). As her next love was documentary film, she began temping at a bank on Wall Street and volunteering at a documentary production company. The system worked pretty well, so she bounced around volunteering in as many production companies as she could, getting to know people in the industry. At one of her gigs, one of the producers encouraged her to explore international film distribution, since she spoke Italian and Spanish. She didn't even know the industry existed, but he was right, it was an excellent fit for her skills. She started with a small company and hasn't left distribution since; she just flipped sides, selling international programs in the United States. Lisa spoke to us about what drives her career and her success.

What was the key driver to your success?
Content has always been the driver. I have to feel a connection to the program that I am selling. I can't sell widgets; I have to feel good about what I sell and I also have to like and respect the people with whom I work. One time an Australian company was courting me and we ran into each other at a convention. The first question they asked me was what trades I enjoyed reading. I knew instantly they weren't the people for me.

You've been in only four different organizations. How did you know when it was time to make a change?
The first one was easy. There were only two of us and nowhere for me to go. I had to move on to get more responsibility. I stayed there four years and then began networking. It turned out that a woman who I worked with for a very short time at my first production was friends with someone *who was friends* with someone who was the head of a British production company opening an of-

fice in New York. I had to take a step down and act as her assistant, but I was happy to do that as long as I could have my own clients and grow. Much to her surprise, I really committed to the administrative portion of the job and honored my bargain.

And it paid off. I had a great mentor who is actually still in my life, and she took care of me. In six years there I went from manager to director and continued to take on more responsibility, bigger accounts, new business, new markets, and all of the selling. And when the company was sold, I was the one who was kept on.

The company was soon disbanded, so from there I went to work for one of my clients, a mid-sized production and distribution company that hired me to start up their New York office. I worked there for three years until the parent company had financial trouble and I was out of work.

I interviewed with my current employer, but the position they were looking to fill was too junior for me, so I offered to work there on a project basis if they needed any additional sales help, and lo and behold a position became available.

What have been your biggest career challenges?
Learning how to delegate and trusting that other people will do the job the way I think it needs to be done. I got over it by forcing myself and hiring the right person. I started this business as a one-woman show and got used to doing everything myself. The workload became such that I couldn't hang on to everything. Once you have someone you trust it's much easier, although I'll admit I am still a nag.

At some point along the way, did you make a plan for a career?
Do you want me to say yes? No, not really. The key for me was recognizing what I enjoy doing and what I don't. I have a good reputation and created good relationships, and that's what brings the opportunities.

make contact

selling yourself (without selling out)

We laugh when we hear women say, "I won't sell." You might as well say, "I won't breathe," because the reality is that you are always selling. You may not be earning commission, but in both your professional and personal lives, you are always selling—your ideas, your point of view, and your personality. Selling is the whole ball game, so girls, grab a bat.

Selling is not easy and it's not natural. Women are socialized to be humble about their accomplishments. You're taught that if you're a good girl and do good work, people will notice and you'll be rewarded. Wouldn't it be great if that were true?

We've all been there, sitting in that staff meeting hearing a coworker (often male) tell the team how they "made it happen," or "saved the day," or "exceeded all expectations." You rolled your eyes at the time, but fast-forward a day, a week, or a month and that same blowhard is rewarded with a big fat promotion. Why? The blowhard was selling his accomplishments to the people who were able to reward him.

Whether you're looking for a promotion, a new job, a new career, or just networking, selling yourself well will be the key to your success. This chapter will give you all the tools you need to package your accomplishments and increase your confidence. Each day in the workplace you will be selling your ideas to your clients, your team, and your management. With your newfound ability of "the ask," you will be selling more and more every day. Selling yourself is a full-time job.

sales training: it will help

Sales training is big business. Sales theories abound. Current thinking points to moving away from words like "sell" and "close" toward "offer" and "accept." You can buy tapes, attend seminars, and hire consultants. When you type "how to sell" into an amazon .com search, 13,688 books are found. That's a lot of choices and a lot of techniques. As publicists and authors, we sell all the time, but we've never had any formal training. Our advice to improve your sales is pretty straightforward: know your product (you), know what your target needs, and show them the benefit of matching the two up. In publicity, it's easy. When a client publishes a new book or introduces a new product, this is news that we want the media to cover, so we send pitch letters and make follow-up calls. Our "targets" need content—magazines need recipes and pictures, and television shows need great talent, so when Jamie Oliver comes to the United States to promote a book, for example, we "sell" his time to the television shows and he goes on and demonstrates a recipe. Just because money isn't changing hands doesn't mean we're not selling.

But this is just the business of publicity. What about your business of selling, whatever it is? Learning your sales lessons well will help you with all aspects of your career building. Organizations hire and promote people who can sell.

So what do we really need to know? We asked one of our favorite entrepreneurs and consumers of sales training, Chrisi Colabella, president of Construction Information Systems, to share her learning with us. Since Chrisi took over her sales department in 2000, gross revenues have increased 27.22 percent per year and 190 percent over the total seven-year period. Unlike us, Chrisi seeks out training. She loves reading self-help books and listening to sales training tapes, and has made a pretty big dent in the thirteen plus thousand books that are offered on Amazon. Over the years she's culled the good advice, tested it on her team, and put the best stuff into practice. We asked her to share her learning with us, so herewith: "Chrisi's Lessons in Successful Selling." Notice how all of this sales training easily applies when the product is *you*.

chrisi's lessons in successful selling

1. **Work backward.**
   - A prospect is a potential client, customer, or purchaser. It's also a potential job or opportunity. To prospect means to try to unearth new opportunities. Sales is a numbers game. The best salespeople know how many presentations they need to get an order, and how many phone calls they need to make to get an appointment to make a presentation. It works like this: if you need to make five presentations to generate one order and you need to make ten calls to generate one presentation, then you need to make fifty calls per day to generate one order.
   - When you are looking for a job, you will need to send out many

résumés to generate just a few interviews to get just one job. When you are looking to move up in a company, sell yourself to as many people across as many departments as possible. You are always building your profile within an organization and industry, and the more contacts you have, the more opportunities you can generate for yourself.

- Learn the benefits your product or service (or you!) can provide each prospect you see. Based on those benefits, create a series of questions to ask before or during your presentation that will uncover a need that can be solved with those benefits. This is best-selling business guru, Neil Rackham's **SPIN** selling. You ask questions to: understand your prospects **S**ituation; uncover a **P**roblem they have with the way they are currently doing business; expose the business **I**mplications of that problem (loss of time/money/value/etc.); and therefore create a **N**eed for your own product/service based on the benefits you can provide.

- Applying the lessons of SPIN selling to ourselves is easy: understand the manager or company's situation; find the problem/opportunity for yourself; show them the implications/benefit of hiring you and create a need for them to just say Yes to hiring/promoting/relocating/increasing your pay.

2. **Treat each interaction in the workplace as important.** You never know who can help you down the line.

3. **Be purposeful in everything you do. Ask yourself, "What is my objective?"**
   - Another selling guru, Steve Schiffman, says, "The purpose of the first step is to get to the second step. The purpose of the second step is to get to the third step." What he means is: when

you are telemarketing to make appointments, your purpose is to set an appointment, not sell your product. If you stay focused on that, you'll get more appointments. If you try to sell your service/product over the phone, you'll do it an injustice and potentially lose an appointment. Thus, when you're following up on your résumé, don't try to get the job. Focus on getting the in-person interview, where you will have the opportunity to sell yourself in person. When you're meeting someone for the first time inside or outside your organization, focus on finding out who they are, not how they can help you. Nothing is a bigger turn-off than someone who just wants to know what you can do for them.

· Don't unsell yourself by highlighting what you aren't doing. Focus on what you are doing or have done that makes you the obvious solution to their problem.

· Don't just go to every event given by every association under the sun. Focus on one or two at a time, and make sure they are the right group for you. Set goals for what you want to achieve within that setting. Become active in that group and get the most out of the time you spend there. Once you're entrenched, you can back off a little while still maintaining valuable relationships and then shift your focus to a new group.

4. **Role play.** Practice your telephone calls and interviewing skills with other people before you have the moment. Thinking it through in your head and saying it out loud are two totally different things. Practice it again and again until it becomes natural to you.

A common term in the media world is "the ask," and "the get" follows the ask (which is simply a request for something or someone to do something for you). Asking people for things is never easy, and if you seem uncomfortable with your request, then they are less likely to give you the outcome you want.

5. **Listen to your bosses/clients/prospects.** Try really hard to understand their business and what their needs are so you can solve them together.

6. **Follow up with your clients after the sale.** Make sure they are happy and are getting what they expected. If they are unhappy, address it. Very often you can up-sell an unhappy client. Make them feel secure that you're working for them and you've turned an unhappy client into a lifelong client.

   If you're trying to move up the ladder, touch base with management and champion your accomplishments. Reinforce the fact that they made the right decision to hire or promote you or to even go with your recommendation.

7. **Ask for referrals.** If you feel like you've done a good job for someone, provided a good product or service, you should feel good about asking for referrals for more business. If you want a new job or to change careers, don't hesitate to discreetly check with your clients, vendors, or colleagues about opportunities. Just make sure you can trust them first.

8. **Follow up on referrals.** It is crazy how many people will make a flimsy attempt to prospect a referral. And it's really, really crazy to know how few people don't follow up with the person who referred them, to let them know they appreciate the gesture. People don't like to give out referrals unless they feel very confident that the salesperson is going to do a good job. Always write a thank-you note or e-mail immediately. Follow up with a progress phone call: "Linda is meeting with him on Tuesday, thanks again for the referral." And send a final thank-you note with a gift when someone signs on. We get many repeat referrals that way.

   And if you're a girl like Chrisi who's always looking for more information to help better herself, she recommends reading her all-time favorite book: *Charisma: Seven Keys to Developing the Magnetism that Leads to Success* by Tony Alessandra.

who needs to hear your pitch?

Before you can articulate your sales pitch, you must articulate your objectives. Are you looking to find your first job? Get a promotion? Ask for a raise? Increase the size of your network? Win new business? Sell some goods? Switch careers? Effective sales skills will be vital to achieving any number of goals.

First, identify and write down your long-term goal. Be specific. Set a timeline. This is your goal statement. Then break down all of the steps you need to take to accomplish that goal and list ways of achieving each step. You can and likely will have any number of short-term goals or benchmarks between writing your statement and achieving your long-term goal.

We set a goal to write and publish a book about starting a business. It was a pretty lofty goal, and to achieve it we had to break it down into the smaller steps we needed to accomplish to reach the larger goal. And along the way we had lots of people to sell. From the very beginning, Caitlin had to sell Kim on the project. She had to convince her that we could do it and that we'd be successful. So one weekend she sat down in front of her computer and wrote our seventy-page book proposal. She brought it in and sealed the deal. Then together we had to sell the idea and ourselves to a literary agent so they would want to represent the project. And then the agent had to actually sell the book to the publisher. Do you see all the selling that's going on here?

Think about your career in the same terms. Identify what you want to do and what you have to do to get there—that's your career plan. It may change five, even ten times over the course of your career, but that's okay. As you mature and experience more things, you're better equipped to figure out what you want, but it really helps to craft short- and long-term plans. If anybody had asked us when we were in our first jobs (an operator at an answering service and counterperson in a café/bakery) what we'd be doing in fifteen years, we wouldn't have had a clue.

Caitlin was more organized in her early days—she identified that she wanted to move to New York and work in television production. So she crafted a plan to get herself there. She called everyone she knew in New York and told them of her goal and, one by one, people began sharing their contacts, which led to interviews that landed her a job at the Food Network. Kim was less focused and could think only in terms of what she did *not* want. She would take any job in New York City in the media as long as it wasn't in advertising sales.

selling yourself at an interview

Some of this advice is so obvious we can't believe we have to give it. Yet we do. All of this advice comes from our direct hiring experience in the past two years. Even if you already think you're pretty good at interviews, you can always get better.

- **Arrive five minutes before your appointment.** Not two minutes late. Not fifteen minutes early. We had a publicist on the team who wasn't a good fit and we let her go. Among other problems, she was always late—almost every single day. A couple of weeks after she left, a competitor and friend called for a reference. Our publicist hadn't listed us as a reference, but since the interviewer knew us, she picked up the phone. We had a nice conversation about what kind of environment this publicist would excel in and agreed that she should offer the publicist a second interview. As she was hanging up she asked, "Does she have a problem with lateness? She was late to the interview and it gave me a bad feeling." We told the truth about the publicist's work habits and she didn't get the second interview.

- **Don't chew gum during the interview.** Kim actually did this once in her early days and her potential employer stopped the interview and asked her if she wanted to get rid of the gum because he could see it in her mouth when she was talking. If you're worried about your breath, suck on a mint just before you begin.
- **Dress appropriately.** Look like you made an effort. Suits on men and women suggest that you are taking the interview seriously. Even if you never wear it again.
- **Don't bring coffee or snacks with you.** We had a candidate who sat down at the table with her deli cup of joe and sipped it during the interview. You're not in a café. You're in a job interview.
- **Cover your ink and pull out your piercings.** Even the most liberal employers don't want to see your tattoos. And for God's sake, remove your tongue ring; there is nothing more distracting in an interview than someone clicking their tongue piercing against their teeth.
- **Get your party pictures off www.myspace.com.** Potential employers are savvy about social networking and are checking out your site. Don't give them a reason to worry about you.
- **Do your homework.** We've had more than a few candidates ask us what we did, so we ask ourselves, why are you here?
- **Think before you speak.** One candidate told us the only reason she was interviewing was because she figured it was time to get a real job.

- **Don't ask what a typical day is like, what your holiday schedule is, or what kind of benefits the company offers in the
  first interview.** In the first interview you are selling them.
  They have to sell you when they offer you the job.
- **Don't get caught embellishing your accomplishments or
  references.** One of our employees gave us a reference who gave
  us a glowing recommendation. After he had worked there a
  couple of months we realized that his glowing reference was his
  cousin whom he had briefly worked for. We couldn't trust him
  after that.

selling yourself in thirty seconds or less

According to Wikipedia, "An elevator pitch (or elevator speech) is a
brief overview of an idea for a product, service, or project. The pitch
is so called because it can be delivered in the time span of an elevator ride (say, thirty seconds or 100–150 words)." Elevator pitches
developed during the Internet boom as a way for venture capitalists
to quickly weed through all of the ideas they were being pitched. It's
a great exercise to apply to both yourself and your business.

We all know you get only one chance to make a first impression,
so it makes sense to spend some time perfecting your elevator pitch.
When you're out and about, on a business trip, at an industry function, or even a media interview, a strong and practiced elevator
pitch will make an excellent first impression.

To craft an exciting elevator pitch, answer the following five
questions:

- What is my skill, talent, service, product, company, or cause?
- What problem do I solve (or what demand do I meet)?
- How am I different?

- Why should you care?
- What do I want from you?

An elevator pitch will also be helpful at networking events, or when selling new ideas to management, approaching a potential mentor, pitching a new client, or running into the CEO in the actual elevator!

It sounds easy, but takes some time and thought to perfect. After all, you have to answer all of these questions in one paragraph. We've had a hard time perfecting our elevator pitch for a couple of reasons: we hate to sound like we're bragging and we've got two businesses going and found it tricky to articulate both businesses. When we would share our reluctance with other businesswomen, we got some universally good advice: "Get over it!"

As to which pitch to share, know your audience. Let's assume we're meeting a potential client at an industry event. In the food world, our elevator pitch goes like this:

We're partners in YC Media, a boutique public relations firm specializing in generating media placements for food-focused businesses, including products, talent, books, and retail. In the past six years we've quadrupled our billings, and worked with some of the biggest names in food, securing regular appearances for them on national television and in major publications. We are targeting our growth only on properties where we can generate consistent media results, and we think your project would be a good fit for us. Can I schedule an appointment to present our qualifications?

In our new sales parlance it works this way: to the new prospect, this elevator pitch effectively describes who we are—"partners"—which is important because the prospect knows they are meeting the decision-makers in a "boutique public relations firm" (that says we're small, we do PR, and there are a few more employees) that "specializes in generating media placements" (we're not big events people or promotions people, we generate media placements) for "food-focused businesses" (we specialize in one industry, not like many of our competitors who are generalists). We illustrate our track record and explain where we excel and let them know they are a target of potential business. And then we ask for a follow-up meeting.

10 WAYS TO STAY POSITIVE WHEN YOU KEEP HEARING "NO"

1. Rework the pitch. Many times in our careers, all it took to get a "yes" (after a series of nos) was rephrasing our request.
2. Focus on the solutions, not the problems. There are always going to be challenges. Put your energy into overcoming them, not wallowing in your setbacks.
3. Champion the accomplishments of others. Enthusiasm is infectious and it feels good to spread good news.
4. So you made a mistake. We all do. What did you learn from it? Don't repeat past mistakes. Focus on what you've learned and how you can apply your lessons to the next situation.
5. Fake it. That's one thing everyone will agree women do well. Enough said.
6. Confront an uncomfortable situation quickly and head-on. Time will not make it better—most likely it will get worse.
7. Be your own biggest fan. If you don't believe in yourself and your ideas, no one else will.
8. Know your stuff. It's much easier to be positive about an outcome when you know what you're doing. The flip side is know what you don't know; don't be afraid to ask questions or seek opinions from outside experts.

9. Go for a single. Very rarely will you hit a home run your first time at bat. Even without the sports analogy the message works. You don't need to always aim for the big accomplishment. Stringing together a series of smaller accomplishments will get you to the same place, and you get the added benefit of all of the little wins along the way.

10. Things really do have a way of working out. When you're in the throes of a stressful situation, it's hard to believe, but have a little faith.

girl taking charge

JEANNE MARIE SCURA, COMMISSION SALES

Jeanne Marie Scura is a happily married mother of three girls and the most successful saleswoman we know. She's been in the fashion business for twenty years and currently is a vice president at Vanilla Star Jeans, where she created and runs the kids' division of this start-up denim company. She's also a heavily commissioned sales rep.

Jeanne Marie loves clothes. She worked her way through New York City's Fashion Institute of Technology, first going full-time during the day and spending summers working in the buying office of The Children's Place. She then found a full-time job at Ocean Pacific, right down the street from FIT, as an assistant sales rep and worked during the day while continuing her education at night.

Jeanne Marie has had a knack for being at the right place at the right time in her career. She worked at OP during its heyday. It was the eighties and beach clothes were hot. She stayed there for five years, being promoted first to the mart manager—which meant she worked on salary, running the showroom and managing the sales reps for the corporate office until she gained enough experience to get her own accounts (and her first commissioned position). She started with the mom and pop specialty stores and then moved up to larger regional chains.

The fashion business operates like many other businesses in that new companies start up and, if they're successful, grow and grow, building brand equity, until they are sold to big corporate entities that license off their divisions. So went OP, and Jeanne Marie moved on to Bum Equipment as a salesperson handling men's and boy's. She worked there for five years, riding their success. It was the kind of environment where you didn't have to be much of a salesperson to be successful—the sales force was little more than order takers, as at the time BUM couldn't ship enough product. But all good things come to an end and BUM was sold, and Jeanne Marie moved on again.

This time she went to work·with Georges Marciano (the disgruntled other Marciano brother who left Guess in a dispute) to start Yes, a company that was supposed to bring down Guess. When that didn't work, she moved to another start-up, Body Code, all the while gaining experience, confidence, and a reputation in the market as a denim expert. Body Code was lackluster and she moved on to LEI, a denim company where she enjoyed a good run for two years until she left to start up the kids' division at the new kid on the block, Mudd Jeans.

At Mudd, she enjoyed a small base salary and a generous commission package. For startups it's the only way to go—if you don't sell, you don't get paid, so nobody can lose. At Mudd she had 100 percent control over the product. She oversaw design, merchandising, production, costing, and of course sales. She started at zero and built it up over eight and a half years to a $60 million business. Mudd has since been sold to the big corporate bores and Jeanne Marie is starting over again.

She shares her insight and wisdom about the competitive world of commission sales—the all-risk, all-reward, cutthroat venture that she's made her career for the past twenty years.

What's the secret to success in sales?
To be successful in sales you need to be a good product person and have confidence. If I've gotten the product right, then I'm con-

fident that when I make my sales call it's communicated to the buyer and they give me an order. Confidence takes time and experience to build.

The great thing about doing this for so long is that I have built relationships in the industry because my product has a good track record. So I'll get a second order and a second chance to get it right. Sometimes it's as easy as changing a thread color in the stitching, and sometimes I have to start over from scratch.

Confidence isn't something that can be taught. I work with other salespeople who I think are very good, but they always seem a bit nervous. They don't trust themselves and their product, and the buyers can see it. If we present the same line to the same buyer, I will always get a bigger order and that's because I really believe in what I am doing.

At this point in my career, the buyers trust me to deliver the right product, but before I had total control over what I was selling (now I'm involved in the design and production of every piece of clothing I sell), I'd be given a ton of crap and would have to make something with it. Of the forty styles that they would hand me, I would edit it down until I found looks that I felt good about selling. Because if I went into a presentation with bad product or unprepared, the buyers would tear me down.

Right now I am working on developing my private label business, which targets clients I have never worked with before. Sure, my reputation is a help, but my confidence is what makes me successful. I walk into these appointments knowing that if they don't use me, then they are missing an opportunity and it's their loss. It's a lot like a first date: if a guy sees that you're nervous and desperate, he's not going to be interested. If you can project that you can take it or leave it, then you probably have a better shot.

Experience gives you confidence.

a view from the ladder

Marcella Regniault describes herself as much more tortoise than hare. Well, maybe if the tortoise was forced to race up a swift-moving stream. Marcella has been fighting the current in the corporate world of Time Inc. for almost twenty years, slowly but assuredly building relationships above, below, and next to her which helped her create an incredible career.

Marcella was born in Italy and raised in Sunset Park, Brooklyn an Italian girl in a traditional Italian immigrant family. Marcella went to a SUNY school and was expected to become a nurse or a teacher. She always knew she was smart, dependable, hardworking, and motivated by learning new things. She also has a knack for developing and nurturing relationships with people in all levels of an organization. She treats the guys in the mailroom the same way she treats the president of the company. After all, she notes of the mailroom guys, "I know those guys. I come from the same neighborhood."

She's currently the executive director, ad operations and planning, for SI Digital. She runs a department of ten people and loves her job. It wasn't an easy or fast ascent, but now that Marcella is at the top, she shares with us the path she took and how all along the way she had to sell her talents to management, human resources, and maybe most importantly to herself.

What was your vision for your career?
I really didn't have one. I've always known I'm a turtle, not a hare. I like to learn new things and am a quick study. My motivating factor has always been happiness—I didn't focus on a title or money. I wanted to work for and with smart people. I am stimulated by them and thrive in that environment. I was never driven by ambition. And I still don't think I am really.

Yet, you're an executive director at a major media company?
Yes I am, but I certainly wasn't groomed for the role. I started out as an "admin" in 1988, and you must remember it was a different

world back then. An "admin" is essentially a secretary and once you were on that track, you stayed there.

You mean like *Working Girl*?
A lot like that, I am afraid. When I was in my first admin job, I noticed that my boss had a very hard time keeping a staff, especially women. They quit pretty soon after they started. I saw an opportunity for myself and went in and asked my boss for a shot. I figured I couldn't be worse than the people who quit. He turned me down—in the most patronizing way possible. He told me that I was "much too important in my current role" to be considered for a promotion.

How did you get around that attitude?
It's funny, I'm not sure I got around it actually. I just outlasted it. I transferred to a sales assistant position for the company in Detroit and worked there for another four years. When I came back to New York, I picked up where I left off in my former job for that same boss. I had increased responsibilities, but I knew I had to make a move.

How did you make the move?
I would never use the word networking, and don't consciously network; however, I have excellent relationships with the people I work with. I also know how to get things done. I recently discovered that at every job I've been in the standard line was "if you need something, go to Marcella; she'll get it done." After another year in the admin job, I sent an e-mail to the nicest guy I knew in sales, who was making a move to the online side. I asked him if anything opened up to please let me know. Within a week, there was a job available and I applied for it.

That sounds great. You're finally taking control of your career.
It would have been great except that when I went to Human Resources, a girl younger than me, by the way, told me that I wasn't qualified for the job and I probably shouldn't bother applying. I applied anyway and got the job and made the big jump to the online side as a sales development associate.

What was that job like?

At online, things move so fast. You're always adapting for the new technology or idea, and if you can't do that then you are definitely in the wrong place. It was also fun. Everybody was really young and once again I developed a reputation as someone who could get things done. I also realized that the dot-com bust was coming, so before it did, I reached out to my colleagues at SI.com (I was at Pathfinder then) and got a new job as a marketing associate.

Did you really make another lateral move?

Yes I did. I had a good reputation internally and really leveraged that. I worked hard and became indispensable to the group.

When did you realize you should be working at a higher level?

The head of sales at SI.com told me that I knew more than anyone in the room in the meetings I was attending and I should speak up. I guess I had a confidence issue, but it never occurred to me that I should speak up, even though I knew I knew more. And after I started speaking up, I never looked back. I got tired of hearing if you want something done go to Marcella and not having a title and compensation that matched my reputation and work product. I was then promoted to manager and then again pretty quickly to a director.

Your management noticed and rewarded you? That's rare.

It wasn't exactly like that. I lobbied for my director title. One day I looked around and realized that I was managing more people than anyone else. I drafted a detailed e-mail with my request for promotion, and after ten months of negotiating I was promoted. Five years later, they made me an executive director.

If you had it to do over again . . .

It's easy to say I would have gotten on a career track sooner, but remember, it was a different culture twenty years ago. Being an assistant now is a career path, back then it wasn't. You get more confident as you get older, and I hope I would have trusted myself and spoken up sooner. I knew I was good and people liked and depended on me. I just never used that to my advantage as much as I probably could have—or certainly as much as others have done.

What are your lessons for girls today?

I really try to mentor the crop of associates who seek my advice. I am really proud that the people whom I have trained are doing really well and I give them all the same advice: be a sponge. Pay attention to every situation and learn from it. Even if it's horrible, focus on what you can take away from it—even if it's only "I'll never do it that way." I concentrate on treating other people the way I would have wanted to be treated when I was coming up. I reward people for good work and encourage them to pursue opportunities to take on more responsibility and make more money.

the new girl's network

You now have a clearer idea of where you want to go with your career and a handle on selling yourself (or at least are moving in the right direction), so you must start thinking about how to make it happen. The next step is cultivating a vibrant network of people to help you move forward and reach your goals. We often forget that networking with other women offers incredible opportunities for career growth.

The Old Boys' Club is alive and thriving and doesn't benefit women at all. Girl's Guide believes that it is a responsibility of women to help other women. We don't mean only hire women, but rather it is essential that we make ourselves available for those who are seeking our career advice. Too often we sell our experience, our professional story, short. We forget that what we have to say and what we have gone through to get to this place in our careers may help other women just starting out. In this chapter we will talk to mentors, entrepreneurs, and board members about how women can give back and create a support system comparable to the one that men have benefited from for years.

creating a new girl's network

In past generations, men have mastered networking in myriad ways. Colleges, clubs, sports, even brothels were used to build up relationships among men that were used to further their careers. Women have been steadily building up their own networks, but still it seems that too often we are enemies in the workplace and not advocates. We don't share our professional stories with other women because we think no one wants to hear them. We don't seek out mentors because we are afraid of getting turned down. Many of us avoid women's conferences, not seeing the importance of spending a day hearing from and talking to other women. Or worse, we don't see the value in it. Only when we do build our own networks and contribute *to* and rejoice *in* the successes of other women will we be on an even playing field.

You need to get into a mind-set that is geared to helping women by being a supportive and honest voice for those around you. Our book club is made up of eight women, in a range of professions from television production to construction. Over the five years that we have been meeting, our group has evolved into a support group of sorts. We spend a little time talking about the book we read, a little time talking about our loved ones, and a lot of time talking about work. Each one of us inevitably comes to the table with a career issue to be discussed and dissected by the group. We have encouraged one another to quit jobs, to take jobs, and to start our own businesses. We encourage each other to speak up, to ask for things, and to make more money. A little *Da Vinci Code*, a little red wine, a little empowerment . . . that's a New Girl's Network.

Other ways to build your network:

- Join professional organizations
- Check out online communities focused on your field
- Attend conferences, seminars, and workshops
- Become active in local government
- Say "yes" when asked for advice or guidance
- Start up a professional support group for women with similar issues: within your industry, for women just getting started, or for working moms in your area

Most important, make it a priority for you to help other women succeed. It makes you feel good, you are generating goodwill that will come back to you in some way (hello Karma!), and it's the right thing to do.

how not to network

Over the past year we have experienced some very poor networking techniques—so bad, in fact, that they offered great "how not to" lessons for this book. Here are two recent exchanges that we have had with those looking to add us to their contact list.

1. "HELP, I WAS JUST NETWORKED!"

Caitlin was working on this book at a neighborhood restaurant when she was approached by a man whom she had noticed working on his laptop nearby. They had shared a brief polite smile, but she was surprised a few minutes later to find him standing over her with his outstretched hand.

"Hi." They shook hands.

"Hello."

"So, what do you do?"

"Um . . ." Caitlin was thrown by the question. Sure, she's always curious about what people do for a living but was taught to not accost people with the question.

"I co-own a public relations business and I write business books for women."

The man went on to tell her about his sportswear design company and she found herself enjoying the conversation until . . . "So did you read the Style section over the weekend?"

For those of you who don't read the *New York Times*, the Style section comes out every Sunday and highlights topics such as fashion, parties, high society, weddings, basically everything that is trendy in the city.

"Because there was an article in there about this." He waved his hand indicating both of them.

"This?"

"Yes, this. The networking thing. Over breakfast. Apparently very hot right now." He gave Caitlin his card.

"I'm Michael."

They shook hands for a second time.

"So coffee. I'll touch base with you."

And just like that, Caitlin had been "networked." But there were so very many things wrong with Michael's style.

- Don't tell someone you're networking even if you are. Networking should be a somewhat organic exchange between two people who like each other or at least have a lot in common professionally. If you don't click personally, it just won't go anywhere. It's like dating—you know there's the possibility of sex, but you don't talk about it.

- Don't start out asking someone what they do. That should never be the only thing that defines you, and if someone is focused only on your career, it leaves you feeling pretty cold.
- Introduce yourself when you meet someone new, not five minutes into a conversation.
- If it is clear that you have zero in common professionally (business books for women and a sportswear design company?), then don't say that you'll follow up. You both know that just isn't happening.
- People respond to authenticity, so be yourself.

2. "HEY, GIRLY, KARMA IS BOOMERANG."

Out of the blue Kim had gotten an e-mail from Jenn, a young lady who had read our books and was looking for some career guidance. Kim immediately got back to her and arranged to have coffee. It turned out that while Jenn was successful in radio sales, what she really wanted was a job in public relations, but she wasn't sure how to go about it. Kim agreed to review her résumé, suggested ways that she could break into the field, and even passed her name along to a few people.

The protégée soon landed her dream job and sent a thank-you e-mail. Less than a month later, we realized that her story would be the perfect addition to this book. She was able to transition into a completely different career in less than six months, so surely she would have advice to share. Kim contacted her about an interview and she immediately said "yes" but then disappeared. We went back to her to schedule a time to talk. After a few days we got an e-mail from her that simply said, "Sorry, too busy. Good luck with the book."

This was very poor form.

- If someone has taken the time to mentor you, if they ask you for help, try your best to follow through.

- Building a useful network means maintaining relationships. Once this woman landed the job, she should have made keeping in touch with us a priority, if only because if this job didn't work out we could help her find the next.

advice for building a vibrant and useful network

Once you have developed your professional goals, it's easier to know who to approach and incorporate into your network. You want to be building a group of people who will work to help you get where you want to be. If your dream is to break into a new industry, you need to work toward meeting people in the jobs that you want to know more about.

Erin Keating, cofounder of Broad Collective, a support and networking organization for women artist-entrepreneurs, shares this:

> Think of networking as talking to like-minded people about the things you're passionate about, and finding out what they're passionate about. What's sleazy about that? Seek out new relationships at every turn. Be who you are, not who you think you should be. You will find your people, and your people will help you. Some people will not be your people; accept that, make peace with it, and move on.

Invest time and energy into your people. If you're building a group of contacts that you can help and that can help you, it's important to stay connected. And not just with the occasional e-mail. Having lunch, grabbing a cup of coffee, any opportunity for a face-to-face will go far in strengthening the personal connection.

Keep it current. You should have a network of people for all phases of your career. Erin Keating continues, "In every phase of my career, relationships have opened doors that seemed locked, helped me build on past experiences, allowed me to practice talking about what I want to achieve professionally, given me solace, support, and insight, and made the next step possible."

Keep an eye toward the future. Gone are the days of pensions and lifetime employment. Don't be afraid to work it: even after you've landed your dream job, keep building relationships and expanding your network. Let your community know what you're up to. Go to conferences and events—if you can position yourself as an expert, speak on panels or judge events. Keep talking about your *big* dream and being your authentic self. Keep looking for your people and taking them out to lunch. Every step is just a step on the journey, and everyone you meet along the way can play a part in your success down the road (as you may play a part in theirs).

Network internally and externally. You want a broad range of contacts to reach out to. For obvious reasons it is essential to build a support group within your company. But not so obvious are the benefits to developing contacts on the outside. First, it expands your knowledge about your industry if you can ask questions and advice from people at other companies. Second, if you are ever at the point of needing to or wanting to leave your current company, you will have people to reach out to.

what is mentoring?

We'll start by saying what it isn't. Mentoring is not giving out occasional advice. It isn't holding back information. It isn't using information that is told to you in confidence to further your own career. Mentoring requires selflessness, like making yourself available even when you have only one free lunch for the next month. It requires honesty and openness and the understanding that this person is counting on you for both. The best mentors are ones who are invested in your success, who share their contacts and opportunities with you. Mentors share their experiences and advice whenever it is needed. They have no agenda other than to help their protégée become the best they can be in their chosen profession. Mentoring is another great way to build your network over time, as eventually your protégées will rise to become players in their field—and an excellent source of help to you.

Whom you should mentor

Should you decide that you are ready to mentor someone, keep in mind that the individual has to be someone you like and respect. They should be someone you want to see succeed. Since you are going to invest time and energy in helping this person, then they need to share your point of view, moral fiber, and goals. If you are approached by someone who asks you to mentor them, don't say yes immediately. Sit down with them and discuss where they want to take their career. Ask them what role they envision you playing and what they would expect from you. You need to set boundaries about your availability in the beginning, being clear about what you can share and what you can't. If you are someone whose business relies on your contact list and that is what they are looking for, then it isn't going to work out.

Whom you should not *mentor*

It isn't a good idea to mentor someone who is clearly going after your job or your business. It isn't a good idea to mentor someone when there is too much professional baggage between you. For example, if a former assistant who had been a disappointing employee approached you and asked you to mentor her, stay away. We had a strange situation with a former employee who would ask our advice frequently, including pointed questions about how we priced our public relations services. Over the course of a year, she had contacted most of our clients to pitch her own business, going so far as to hire our Web designer and use our corporate colors to promote her own business. So be open, but also be careful with this relationship—with the wrong person, you could be making yourself professionally vulnerable.

When you should run from a mentor relationship
Run for the hills when . . .

- **It's an <u>All About Eve</u> situation.**
  Is she mimicking your professional style a bit too closely?
- **She is asking too many detailed questions about your business.**
  Does she really want your proprietary information like clients or contacts?
- **Her business is too close to your own.**
  If there could be a conflict of interest at some point, stay away.
- **She has an agenda, such as wanting your job.**
  Try not to get into a mentoring situation with someone who is angling for your office.
- **There is an emotional layer to the relationship.**
  If she is a friend, former romantic partner, or even a friend of a friend . . . take a pass.
- **There is professional baggage that could come into play.**
  Did she used to work for you or you for them? Was she passed over for the promotion that was given to you? If there is any complexity to the relationship, then you will not be able to give or receive objective advice and support.
- **There is jealousy lurking.**
  Be honest with yourself. There are people who inspire jealously. Maybe they are creative in a way you always wanted to be. Maybe they are an amazing writer; maybe they have mastered

public speaking while it continues to be a challenge for you. Or maybe you have felt that in some way they are jealous of you. Be aware and honest with yourself about those people who on the surface seem a perfect professional match but you just can't put your finger on why it feels uncomfortable. It could be jealousy.

Finding your own mentor

We had a hard time finding a mentor. Our first mentor was a woman who was in our industry but not in our specific area of business, so we felt comfortable asking her for guidance when we faced staffing issues, client problems, and growing pains. Although we always appreciated the time she gave us, after a few years we realized that we had outgrown her advice. It's important to know, as with any relationship, that there could come a time when you have moved beyond what this person can offer you.

Our second mentor was a former consultant who we had the utmost respect for. But when we started diving into the details of our business with her, it became obvious that she was so committed to the way she ran her own business that she was unable to accept that it was okay that we did things differently.

What we learned after a few rocky attempts to find and foster the perfect mentor relationship is that you don't have to have just one. You can actually benefit from several mentors with differing levels of experience and diverse expertise. You also need to know that you may outgrow a mentor, and that's OK.

If you're lucky, your boss will be a mentor figure for you. Josianne Pennington, now one of the principals of Full Bloom Strategic Marketing & Events, started her career at a major Fortune 100 company. "After a few months at the job, I was promoted and I really hated the new position. I would spend hours at my desk analyzing numbers, not a great use of my natural skills or ability, but I felt I had to stay there in order to justify their faith in me. After a few months I finally went to the head of the company and asked what I could do to better position myself for a role in the company that I felt I was better suited for. What I didn't realize at the time was that I had just gone out and found myself a mentor. My boss started inviting me to meetings outside my direct area and would occasionally ask for my input. I knew that by making my feelings known in a positive, proactive way I was positioning myself for the next move, which would come sooner than later because I had just spoken up." For Josianne, the lightbulb moment was twofold: find a mentor and don't be afraid to speak up on your own behalf.

Vicky S. Wu, CEO and founder of Froghop, Incorporated, a full-service solutions provider for transmedial needs, believes strongly in the role of mentors, having benefited from this type of relationship herself. "I love mentors, because they become a champion for you." But she advises that you need to approach these potential mentors with respect. "I let them know why I'm interested in getting to know them, what I admire about them, and what I am looking to learn from them. You have to really prove to them in a very short amount of time why they should spend additional time with you." Since you are reaching out to someone who knows more than you or is above you on the ladder, then assume that they have precious little time. So you need to sell yourself a little when you meet with them and demonstrate that you are worth spending time on.

5 WAYS TO SOCIAL NETWORK

1. Woody Allen said it best: "Eighty percent of success is just showing up."
2. Sign up for online social networking sites. Two good ones to start with are www.oomph.net and www.linkedin

.com. As with everything else, these sites give back only what you put in. You have to dedicate time to building up your pages and updating your profile. Check out this tool to help you "trick out" your page: http://www.picgames .com/forum/myspace-layout-editor.php.

2. Join industry organizations. Old school still works, and the most efficient places to meet people who will help you move along in your career are industry organizations. Joining is not enough. To maximize the benefits, you must get involved with the group. Attend the meetings and functions, work on committees, or maybe run for office.

4. Join a social group. When our friend Chrisi Colabella moved to a new town, she joined the "working mom's play group" organized by her county. It was a great place to meet women who were sharing a similar experience if not a similar industry.

5. Take a class or attend a seminar. Not only is the curriculum valuable, but meeting the other students and faculty is an easy way to expand your network.

women who share

We can learn a lot from each other. One of the reasons we love writing these books so much is because the women we interview share their experiences—good and bad. Sharing your successes and failures helps others think about themselves and their lives differently. We make an effort to tell people about the time we blew an interview, hired an employee for all the wrong reasons, or made fools of ourselves on national television. We also tell people about our experience publishing the Girl's Guide books. Why? Because we want women to know that if *we* can do it, warts and all, they can too. And the most satisfying part of our experience is hearing from the women who were encouraged by our honesty to take a professional chance. So don't discount your experiences, don't downplay your successes, and always be open when someone is asking you how you got where you are. Because who knows who you will inspire along the way?

We were once told by Suze Orman that in order to connect with people, it's important to share your story. She was talking specifically about public speaking, but we think that this applies to relating in general. We learn from one another's stories because we see ourselves in the choices of other people, and we can avoid mistakes if someone has already made them. If you ask questions of the women you meet—and you in turn open up about your career path—you never know what someone is going to learn. You could be inadvertently changing someone's path.

As the founder of Kim Ricketts Book Events, Kim Ricketts frequently has the opportunity to hear great women leaders speak about their experiences. She told us that there have been at least two stories that changed the way she thought about herself. The first was Madeleine Albright. "When she spoke about staying home with her daughters until they were in school, then getting her first job when she was forty-two(!), I felt so hopeful that after staying home with my children, I could achieve my dream of being an entrepreneur. After all, look how far Ms. Albright went with her career!" The other was Carly Fiorina, former CEO of Hewlett-Packard. "When she talked about people who pursue and embrace change she referred to them as 'change warriors' because she recognized how hard it is for these people who move us forward and that 'they fight a war every single day.' This was so validating for me, since I can get exhausted trying to create a new kind of business in a very traditional bookselling culture."

those who do should also teach

Even if you are swamped and your to-do list is killing you, give back a little of your expertise when asked. We are called for career advice all the time, and always make the time to offer our thoughts. Kim Ricketts is great at this.

I have met with many women who want to start companies similar to what I do and I give them all the history, ideas, and information I can to get them started, as I believe that by giving you will always get more. People tell me I should not give away my business secrets and ideas, but I always say "we have to stop thinking about how thinly we are slicing the pie, and instead make more pie!" I truly believe that the more successful women there are, the easier it will be for everyone to succeed.

BY WOMEN FOR WOMEN

Slowly women are ascending the ranks of management and assuming leadership positions in organizations across the country. Progress, sure, but not enough for many of us and so we opt out to start our own businesses. The latest trend shows women not just starting businesses but targeting their businesses to women too. Here are three companies taking the New Girl's Network to the next level.

See Jane Work
Tired of seeing the same old, boring products? So was See Jane Work founder and CEO Holly Bohn. "There is only so much you can do with smoke-colored plastic trays," she exclaimed. "There must be another way!" After consulting with several friends, she

realized there were stylish office supplies out there; they were just so hard to find. So, www.seejanework.com was born, the online destination for office style and organization.

According to Holly, "Jane is a fictional character who embodies everything working women are today. Whether our work is in the home, in the office, or, in the home-office, we are expert organizers and multitaskers who can lead the staff meeting, make the contract revisions, and schedule the vet appointment, all before we've had our second cup of coffee." See Jane Work offers working women, no matter what kind of work they do, the tools to manage their time efficiently, and to get and stay organized in a way that looks great.

See Jane Work has opened a retail store and is now manufacturing See Jane Work–branded products. Holly and her cohort in crime, and best friend since first grade, Vice President Kelly Osborne, have a vision for the company's future that includes retail outlets, a franchising program, and continued new product development. They love championing other women's causes too and have been known to give away great ideas because they want all women to benefit.

Golden Seeds

After working for years in the men's world of high finance, and watching women's businesses get overlooked, the women of Golden Seeds (www.goldenseeds.com) decided to pool their girl money power and help women-owned businesses utilize both their intrinsic and financial capital to achieve their full potential. Golden Seeds identifies and invests in women-led ventures with the potential to grow into multimillion-dollar businesses. Golden Seeds offers money and, perhaps more important, guidance to women business owners so they can achieve their goals.

We met Executive Director Erica Duignan Minnihan in the green room of MSNBC's *Your Business*. Erica spent the first fifteen years of her career in the world of finance, working for many of the big institutions. Prior to joining Golden Seeds, Erica was an asset-backed securities trader with the fixed income division of Cantor Fitzgerald. She also worked for Citigroup and Credit Suisse

First Boston in the investment banking and asset management divisions. She received her M.B.A. in finance and real estate with honors from Columbia University and a B.A. in business economics from the University of California at Los Angeles. In her new role as executive director of Golden Seeds, Erica evaluates hundreds of proposals a month from women business owners all over the country looking for investment capital.

girl taking charge

Because she has learned so much from mentors and goes out of her way to take on that role in other people's lives, we spoke to Vicky S. Wu, CEO and founder of Froghop, Incorporated, about the benefits to having that relationship in your life.

Where did the impetus to find mentors come from?
My mom always told me to "be smart about things." Even though it's OK to make mistakes, you don't have to make every mistake yourself in order to learn. She taught me to observe others. Don't reinvent the wheel every time. Learn from others, figure out whether and how it applies to your own life, and adjust as necessary.

How did mentors help you become successful?
They helped me be more efficient by relaying "tried and true" techniques so I didn't have to stumble through and figure it out all by myself. I think it's important to not blindly take the advice and apply it without thinking how your circumstances are different, but as long as you are aware of that, they can save you time. Even if once in a while the advice they gave "wasn't right," I was able to figure out what was right for me a lot quicker through the thought process of why that advice wasn't right in my shoes.

They also helped me save a lot of money. To start with, the advice I got was free. I got top-quality advice that others would've had to pay through the roof to get. One of my mentors did some consulting for a while, and his billing rate was approximately $300 an hour! As an entrepreneur, I certainly couldn't afford that. I also avoided costly mistakes, as I've had a lot of help with strategic planning and ensuring the path was a solid one to go down. I also made more money because they helped me hone my sales pitch and polish my sales closes, and I have even had them accompany me on large important deals.

Through believing in me and being my mentor, they gave me access to contacts that I did not have. Sure, I could build them, but that takes time. Through introductions, you get instant credibility and response. That helped for business development, as well as the "building my bio" part. I learned what type of events to go to, how to get noticed, how to get others to come to me, and how to effectively use my extracurricular activities to continue building my bio.

Mentors have helped me grow my business, they have introduced me to people and organizations that I otherwise may not have known and been involved with, they have served as a sounding board. Because of their wisdom and advice, I have developed into a more well-rounded individual than if I were trying to figure life out on my own.

a view from the ladder

As a rule, Superwomen scare us. While inspiring in many ways, the massive success of Martha Stewart and Oprah Winfrey seems not only impossible to achieve but ends up making us feel inadequate. And we wouldn't even try to get access to them. So when you're lucky enough to have gone to high school with one of *Time* magazine's "Top 100 Influential People," who also happens to be a *Newsweek* cover girl, *and* she offers to talk to you about anything you want, you jump at the chance.

Caterina Fake is not only a Superwoman, but a super-cool girl too. She's generous with her time and can be found many nights giving professional advice to strangers who e-mail her. She rarely watches television or sleeps all that much, but she eats information and she's got one of those crazy smart brains—you know, the ones that can do art *and* math. And she's beautiful, by the way, too. But don't hate her.

After a bunch of different jobs in art, graphic design, and even retail, she began designing Web sites and was the art director at Salon.com. From there she moved on to other Web start-ups and then founded www.flickr.com with her husband, Canadian philosopher geek Stewart Butterfield. After sixteen months of a live site, they sold Flickr to Yahoo! for an undisclosed (and we're guessing big) sum.

You can find her now sitting on the board of *Etsy,* advising numerous other start-ups and new businesses and blogging at www.caterinafake.com. At Yahoo! she runs the technology development group, best known for its Hack Yahoo! program, a stimulus to innovation and creativity.

On the eve of jet-setting off to Davos, Switzerland, to speak on a panel with Bill Gates and Google CEO Eric Schmidt at the World Economic Forum 2007, she shared her wisdom about the wonderful and wild world of today's community-driven Internet.

What do we need to know about social networking online?
You can meet amazing people and get fantastic advice online. You can find your next job online, or find mentors online who would probably have been impossible before the Internet. When I'm looking for someone to help me with something, the first thing I do is go to the Internet.

One thing that a lot of people don't realize is that if you put a picture of yourself online, people can download it and save it or it can be stored in something called the Internet Archive, where technically savvy people can access it. As a rule, don't put things on the Internet that you wouldn't want your mom, grandmother, or potential employer to see. The younger generation is much more freewheeling with their privacy than our generation would ever be, so they need to be careful.

But as long as you behave nicely and keep your clothes on, the Net is a great opportunity for networking. You can connect with people directly and find professional mentors.

How do we find people to help us?

The Internet is founded on a culture of generosity. Nine times out of ten, you can find people sharing business advice freely. Whether you're looking for information on business etiquette or details of fashion marketing or opening a restaurant, you can be sure to find something. And many of the people offering advice are happy to be contacted and share more in greater detail.

Start to read individual blogs that are relevant to your field, and when you find ones you like, read them regularly, pay attention to those who regularly respond, and get involved in the conversation. For the most part you are looking for professional business blogs that have good advice. This kind of information can be incredibly useful when you're starting your career, or looking for more information about almost anything. You name the field, there are people out there who can become a mentor in your career.

When we've found the people we want to help us, how do we get them to respond?

People are more likely to respond when you demonstrate that you know what they're writing about and care about their work. You have to show that you're not spamming them. Do your homework. Keep track of their blog and their interests, and when you're ready to contact them, don't be a pest. Some suggestions are:

- Keep your request short. These people are busy and don't have time for your life story.
- Make your request reasonable and something easy for them to do.
- Make sure you include a specific call to action.

For example, an e-mail that I would be more likely to respond to would look something like this: *Hi, my name is Kirstin and I am a* graduate student in Omaha, Nebraska, and long-time reader of your blog. I especially enjoyed [name specific post], and I was hoping you could do a short interview for my research in the next couple of weeks. Below are the questions that I hope you can answer. I'd love to interview you on the phone, but would be thrilled to receive the answers back by e-mail, too.

What if we don't get a response?

Don't take it personally. Most people write a blog so they get to share their views and reduce one-to-one contact. Keep reading, try a few more times, and then move on to someone else. There are lots of people out there who can proffer advice.

What about the "social networking" sites?

Those can be great, and I've used them extensively myself. And these can be useful not just in the obvious ways. If you participate in www.linkedin.com, which is a professional networking site, for example, you don't just meet other people, but you can see the trajectory of their careers in an industry that you want to get into, who they are connected to, and so on.

Should we be out there blogging right now?

Not necessarily. Blogging is a big commitment. If you want to do something to market yourself in a powerful way, you have to be committed to publishing. You must publish frequently and make sure the quality is high. You need to inform, entertain, and be consistent. And in some ways it's better to not have a blog at all rather than a blog that never gets updated. Not everyone can blog every day.

Instead, informational Web sites and standard brochure sites are perfectly legitimate uses of the Web and essential in today's marketplace. People don't go to 411 or the Yellow Pages to find you anymore. They search for you on the Web, and you have to be there.

Say we are committed and ready to blog. How do we make sure our blog gets noticed and gets traffic?

The great thing about the Internet is that the best blogs usually surface and reciprocity is the order of the day. The more attention you give, the more attention you get. The number one way to get more traffic to your blog is by linking with other blogs. Go to http://technorati.com/ and check out the top one hundred or even the top one thousand. Somewhere you'll find blogs that address your subject. Make sure you subscribe to these blogs and read them. There are also dozens of sites that have advice on how to increase your page views and traffic. Read those, but don't get a reputation as a spammer. You will get blacklisted.

But the first thing you've got to have is a well-informed, interesting, educational, and useful blog. Otherwise, any attempts to publicize it will not succeed.

We are old school and we like our networking, social or otherwise, in person. Are we completely out of it? Do we never need to leave our computers?
Of course not. Relationship-building is very important, especially at the beginning of your career, and professional organizations are still excellent places to meet people. Search the Web for the professional organizations that are available in your industry and join them. Go to the meetings, bring your business card, and don't forget to have fun.

PART THREE

rise to the challenges

fear is a four-letter word

When you're trying to do your best, the last thing you want is to be held back by lingering insecurities. In this chapter we're going to confront those head-on so that we can move forward from a place of strength. Believe it or not, many of us undermine our own success. Our fears hold us back. These are the all-too-common fears, like the fear of public speaking, that will directly impact your promotability. If your boss can't ever send you to a conference in her place because you have a fear of flying, how much time/energy/training is she going to invest in you? There are even fears that we are unaware of but hold us back nonetheless—such as avoiding an overbearing but politically powerful coworker or not piping up at the weekly meeting because of a general lack of confidence. And then there is the fear of success. This chapter will identify what might be holding you back and offer tips and advice for tackling the issue.

what are you really afraid of?

Butterflies in the stomach before a new business meeting are common, but you need to be aware of any fears that are actually affecting your chances of more money, a better title, or the perfect job. Below we outline a few fears that the women we interviewed say stalled their careers.

BEING DISLIKED

The fear of being disliked is the most common and most insidious professional fear there can be. Socially, women are driven to be accepted. But in an office environment that drive can be detrimental to your career. If you are focused on staying in everyone's good graces, you won't be able to manage well, ask for what you deserve as far as money or title goes, confront difficult coworkers, disagree with someone during a crucial meeting, stick up for yourself with an abusive client, make a staffing request, fire someone who needs to go, or ask for a high-profile project. If you are worried about people liking you, then you are at their mercy because you won't be able to speak your opinion for fear that it will offend someone.

PUBLIC SPEAKING

We dedicate a chunk of this chapter to public speaking because in most studies it ranks higher than death and disease as our biggest fear. Public speaking is terrifying but something you can master with a little (or maybe a lot!) of effort. Even if you are at the start of your career and infrequently called on to present, it is worth tackling this now because almost all senior positions require some public speaking. If your boss knows that you can confidently and articulately represent yourself, the team, or the company, your career will advance. We know someone who was a marketing assistant at a major magazine. Even though she had only a year of work experience, she was high energy and confident. When the editor in chief asked for a volunteer to appear on a local television show as a spokesperson for the magazine, she jumped at the chance. After the successful interview, she volunteered for any opportunity that put her in the public eye. The magazine so appreciated her skills and enthusiasm that her career was put on the fast track. There are tips on how to become a great public speaker, or at least not faint during the introductions, later in this chapter.

BEING FIRED

Some companies instill this particular anxiety in their staff on purpose to motivate them to do the best job possible. We both worked for a company that made it quite clear that you could be unemployed for loss of a single client. We spent every day we worked there doing whatever we could not to be fired. The fear of no income loomed so large that we never asked for anything and accepted the minimum. Sure, we were motivated to do a good job, but frankly there are healthier ways to get the best from your employees and yourself. Let this fear go and trust that you do a good enough job not to be canned. Here is a management secret . . . you need to be a really bad employee to get fired. Aside from the plethora of legal issues that come into play when you want to fire someone, it also takes a lot of energy, money, and time to train a new staff member and it's just easier to keep whoever you already have.

BEING TOLD NO

We bet that not one of you would say that you enjoyed being turned down. But does your fear of not getting what you asked for stop you from asking? The squeaky wheel really does get the grease, so *not* asking is *not* an option. Sure, you won't always get what you ask for, but sometimes you will. And if your request is responsible, delivered at the right time, and in the right way, then you should get what you want, deserve, and need. We have included tips and suggestions for getting what you need in the "Asking for What You Deserve" chapter.

BEING A BOSS

It is much easier to manage yourself than other people, but you won't go far in your career without the ability to delegate effectively. The key to being a great boss is to be clear with your employees whenever you give them a task. Tell them exactly what it is you need them to do, when it is due, and what your expectations are. Many female bosses are great at building loyalty but are not so great at delegating and end up doing *everyone's* job. Women are great multitaskers, but at the end of the day doing everything is not going to get us a promotion. Building an efficient team of confident employees who take direction and deliver is the road to a corner office.

BEING DOWNSIZED

Every one of us who has worked for someone else has worried about the pink slip. Marie worked at a major network on a television program that was canceled. Although she wasn't fired, she watched six of her coworkers get let go. Soon her paranoia about being fired began taking its toll, and her productivity and enthusiasm for the job plummeted and she ended up quitting. The fact is that you don't have any control over being downsized, so don't let this fear stop you from doing the best job you can. Turn this anxiety into motivation, because the one thing you can control is the quality of your work. If you are a stellar employee, then chances are good that you are building an excellent reputation for yourself. Even if you do get fired, there will be people you can call on for references when you are ready to start looking. If your company is in turmoil or it seems every year you are there is a "down" year, then dedicate even more time to networking on the outside. Join organizations and follow up with the people you meet by taking them to lunch. If you focus on expanding your world beyond your company, you will be in good shape no matter what happens.

BUSINESS TRAVEL

Are you afraid of flying? Are you anxious about being away from your family? Unfortunately, if you avoid business travel it could and most likely will impact your professional development. Even if you own your own business, you may need to travel for a trade show, conference, client, or networking opportunity. If you are worried about being away from your family, then make the trips in as quick a turnaround as possible. We often end up on the red eye so we can shorten the time we are away from home. If it is in fact a medical phobia that is keeping you from getting on a plane, then we recommend that you overcome that as quickly as possible with outside help. If business travel is something you just don't want as part of a new job, be sure to raise the issue in job interviews because it is better to know what you are getting into. If you are thinking about owning your own business, consider partnering with someone who enjoys travel and is willing to do it on your behalf.

the keys to confidence

Have you or do you work with people who exude confidence? Somehow when they come up with an idea in a brainstorm everyone is immediately onboard and when they have an opinion most people agree. Or someone to whom everyone flocks with questions because they always seem to have the answer? These are the people who succeed, because even if they are quaking on the inside, they project a level of confidence that inspires trust. Not all of us are blessed with innate confidence, but we are big believers that if you fake it for a while, eventually you will feel it. Here is some advice we have compiled from women who have done just that.

STAND UP STRAIGHT
Sounds silly, but look around you. How many people are hunching over their computers? How many people walk tall? If you stand up straight, you will be physically projecting confidence even if you aren't feeling it on the inside. Just think of how imposing members of the military look.

PROJECT CALM EVEN UNDER ENORMOUS PRESSURE
Be the person that the team turns to during times of stress and you will be laying the groundwork for a leadership role. The key is to remain calm (real or fake) in the midst of a crisis and provide solutions without contributing to chaos.

LOOK PEOPLE IN THE EYE
Think alpha dog. Strong animals do not back down when someone looks them in the eye. If you are always the one to turn away, then you are subconsciously deferring to the person. When dealing with anyone from your assistant to the CEO, look her in the eye, especially when you are stating a request or opinion.

KEEP YOUR TEMPER IN CHECK
Some people think that yelling shows strength and conviction. But losing your temper actually only demonstrates that you have no control. The really confident people don't need to scream in order to be heard because everyone is already listening.

STAY POSITIVE
We had a coworker who was negative about everything and anything. She thought saying something negative, especially about someone

else's work, would put her in a superior, more knowledgeable position than the rest of us. Instead it made her look completely insecure and uncommitted to her job.

DON'T AGREE UNLESS YOU AGREE
If you want to come off as confident, then you have to be true to your point of view. So when you jump in to back someone up, or pipe in with a "Janet, great idea!," make sure you actually believe it.

CONTRIBUTE YOUR OWN OPINIONS AND IDEAS
Don't just agree or disagree (see above) with your colleagues. If you want to come off as confident, then come up with your own point of view and your own solution to a problem. Since so few people go out on a limb with their own ideas, especially in a group setting, the more you take the risk, the faster you will earn the respect of the team.

HAVE A SENSE OF HUMOR
Who likes the person who can't take a joke? Having a sense of humor, especially about yourself, makes you a more comfortable person to be around. Also, it is only the truly confident people who can laugh at themselves.

BE AUTHENTIC
Your true source of confidence springs from authenticity. That means working for an organization that reflects your values and beliefs, and doing a job that reflects the same. That means that if you own your own business, you choose something that is a natural extension of you; if you ditched art school for a high-paying job but are miserable, you resurrect your creative self. When you find yourself in a completely authentic situation, you will be on the road to real confidence because you will always be able to say "I am a writer,

photographer, sales executive, banker, or graphic designer" with honesty, conviction, and joy.

say it out loud! public speaking

Public speaking is mildly nerve wracking for some of us and terrifying for others. But here is a true statement: you can overcome this fear. Take it from Caitlin. She avoided public speaking for most of her life. She avoided any class throughout both high school and college that required making a speech of any kind. When faced with an unexpected assignment, she would claim that her doctor told her to avoid stress. Her teachers were either taking pity on her or were enabling her, because she gave only one talk in eight years. Soon after graduating from college, however, she found herself at a public relations agency that required each employee to present to the company during the Monday meeting. Since she was a completely inexperienced public speaker, Caitlin spent every Sunday night sick with anticipation. Fast forward: now Caitlin speaks to hundreds, sometimes thousands, of people. She even goes on national television. What happened? She made herself do it, for one. She knew it was a skill she had to master, so whenever an opportunity presented itself, even if it was a talk to fifteen students at a local college, she jumped at it. Although Caitlin still gets nervous, after years of speaking in front of both small groups and large, she is no longer debilitated by her fear. If you do something frequently enough, it just isn't that scary.

Lisa MacGillivray, a public relations and marketing consultant, shares this: "I've had different fears along the way. They've ranged from being fired to presenting and participating in big client meetings. The only way to move past any professional fears is to confront them. If you're nervous about presenting and would rather sit it out, don't. Take the opportunity to work through it and you'll be pleasantly surprised when your nerves stay calm during the next big presentation."

Lisa is right about all of this. The teachers who were letting Caitlin avoid her speeches weren't helping her. If you are someone who avoids speaking—because you are either afraid of looking stupid, being boring, or losing the respect of your coworkers—take a deep breath and do it anyway. Public speaking is a necessity in most professions, but more important, you don't want to harbor a latent weakness that could sabotage your career further down the line. Imagine if you had avoided speaking for years and then suddenly your boss asked you to present in front of the CEO. If you fell apart, it could be all over.

Since it is always better to be prepared, here are a few ways for you to start honing your skills as a public speaker:

KNOW YOUR AUDIENCE

To write a relevant talk, you need to know who you are speaking to. So whenever you are enlisted to present, find out who will be there, why they are coming, what they want to learn from you. No one is asked to speak arbitrarily, so *you* were asked for a reason. What can you share that is important for the group to know?

KNOW THE PROGRAM

Being the closing speaker at an event is drastically different than being the opening speaker, so find out where you fit on the program. Even if you have asked to unveil the new ad your team came up with to the client, find out the flow of the presentation. Along with the subject of your talk, timing and context dictate the tone of a presentation, so ask for those details.

WRITE IT DOWN

Some of us can jump into a speech without writing one in advance. This is a gift. A very rare gift. If you are like the rest of the 99.9 percent of the people in the universe, spend time writing your talk, timing it, and then practicing it. We have tried winging it a few times. Three times it was successful and one time it was a humiliating disaster. So humiliating, in fact, we now follow our own advice.

THE POINT OF POWERPOINT

Not every presentation is better accessorized with audiovisuals. In fact, oftentimes you will get lost if you are the one standing to the left side of a projection screen. We are not fans of PowerPoint, only because after years of being subjected to other people's presentations we have realized that it is actually more interesting to listen to a compelling speaker than to watch images on a screen. People like to connect, and that isn't happening when the attention is focused elsewhere. If you have to use PowerPoint for your presentation, then remember to keep the text brief and whenever possible include photographs, illustrations, or even colorful graphs.

DON'T FORGET TO THANK

If you have been invited to speak by an organization or individual, then it is polite to acknowledge them before you dive in.

A SUCCESSFUL Q&A

If there is a question-and-answer component to the talk, try to plant the first question to get the ball rolling. The first person to pipe in with a question (your plant) helps break the ice for everyone else to jump in with their own.

WHEN YOU BOMB

Sometimes the talk will just go badly. It could be that the energy is off in the room, the attendees are exhausted, or maybe you were just the wrong speaker for the event. We had a disastrous event during our tour for our first book that, while humiliating, offered so many key learnings for us that we now consider it a blessing. Here are just a few of the things we learned.

- **The No-Show**

  The woman who was to introduce us at the talk never showed up. We ended up walking out on the stage to introduce ourselves. Since we could hardly plug ourselves without sounding boastful and annoying, we ended up just stating our names, which did little to position our credibility as experts on the topic.

  Key Learning: Whenever possible, have someone introduce you.

- **Have a Run-Through**

  When we showed up twenty minutes before the talk, we realized that we were going to be on a huge (think Carnegie Hall) stage and that the screen for our PowerPoint was tiny (think slide show in the living room). It was quite obvious once we started that the text was unreadable from the first row (there were fifty rows).

  Key Learning: Find out exactly what the setup of the talk is going to be and work around that.

- **Stories, Stories, Stories**

  Suze Orman was watching our speech and afterward she told us to remember to always share our stories when speaking to a

group. She was right. Even though we were talking about starting a small business, we focused on the how-to instead of
sharing with the group our ups and downs on the road to becoming entrepreneurs.

Key Learning: Whenever possible, personalize the discussion
because it will help you to connect with the audience.

If you have a bomb of a talk, spend time reviewing what happened. It is uncomfortable and painful to revisit an embarrassing
situation, but you might find some nuggets of wisdom that will make
it better the next time around.

push back: don't fear your staff

A few months ago we were asked by *Woman's Day* magazine to mentor a small business owner on her staffing challenges. We found
Peggy Bevan, the owner of The Egg Shell Restaurant in Denver. At
the time of our interview, Peggy was stressed beyond belief, having
just dealt with a mass exodus of waitresses. Peggy had been a stay-
at-home mom for more than thirty years before her husband passed
away. His death forced her back into the workforce, both for money
and something to do. She followed her passion for food and enter-
taining and purchased an existing restaurant. As she put it, "It was a
chance for me to begin a new chapter in my life." While she excelled
at the hospitality part of her business, Peggy had no restaurant or
managerial experience and managing her employees was a challenge. After working with her, we realized she was afraid of them.
She also made a very common mistake: she wouldn't delegate because she wanted things just so. She didn't realize that if she had
taken the time to train them exactly how she wanted it once, she
wouldn't have to worry about it again. Instead, she would scream,

yell, and cry in frustration. She knew that she could do better, so after reading lots of books, speaking to us, and spending time on herself, Peggy now utilizes the great team she has.

Here are a few other lessons we shared with Peggy:

BEWARE OF YOUR TONE

When you are telling your employee to do something, does it sound more like a question than an assignment? If so, then you are asking them *if* and *when* they will do the task. Are you condescending when assigning projects? If so, be aware because that will breed resentment.

MANAGE BECAUSE IT IS YOUR JOB

If you are not directing, guiding, supporting, informing, or inspiring your employees, then you are not doing a good job as a boss.

BE CLEAR

Tell your employees exactly what it is you want them to do, how you want it done, when you want it done by, and (quickly) why you want it done. Leave no room for confusion because that will lead to disappointing results.

IF SOMEONE IS DOING A BAD JOB, LOOK IN THE MIRROR FIRST

It is easy to assume that if someone isn't delivering for you it is their fault—that they are probably all wrong for the job. Well, that isn't true. Perfectly smart, capable people have been fired because they are managed poorly. Look closely at the situation and ask yourself and them if you are giving them everything they need to do a good job.

AN ISSUE WITH YOU BEING A WOMAN ISN'T YOUR ISSUE

Many people have issues with women in positions of power, but frankly, that is their problem. Don't engage in power struggles with your employees. *You* are the boss, *you* call the shots, and *you* have the power to fire them.

DON'T LET THEM ADD TO YOUR LIST

Women are multitaskers, which is a great quality to bring to the workplace until your desire to jump in on everything means that you are adding to your own to-do list. In order to have the time to lead the team well, you need to take things off your plate, not add them on.

We are happy to report that Peggy is thriving in her relatively new role as manager and wanted us to share this with you: "I want your readers to know that it is never too late to start again. I would never have imagined that I would have a new career in my fifties, but I do and it has given me a tremendous amount of confidence. Nothing is impossible if you want it badly enough."

boss from hell: when the problem is above

Unfortunately, your boss doesn't have to change. Even if she is sent to management training and comes back worse than when she left, even if her boss thinks she treats you badly, even if she is clueless. Karen worked for a jewelry store to help pay for college. She knew that her manager was stealing money. He would take cash out of the safe to "hold him over" until payday. Who knew if he ever returned it? He also did this without asking the owner of the store, who lived a state away and was rarely around. He even did this in front of other employees. When Karen mentioned something, he told her to mind her own business. During a visit from the owner of the company, Karen pulled him aside and told him about the manager's habit of "borrowing" money. He nodded his head and said he would consider it. The next day Karen was fired. She was fired because the store was making money and the manager was good enough to allow the owner to live at his lake house two hundred miles away.

The fact is that if the bad boss is delivering for the company, oftentimes that's all that matters. Now obviously we are not talking about sexual harassment or discrimination; if your boss is doing anything illegal, then you need to get Human Resources involved or your boss's boss. But if you work for your run-of-the-mill credit-stealing or temper-losing boss, then you should evaluate whether or not the job is worth it. How important are the skills you are learning in this job to your long-term career growth? Are you being given opportunities or access to information you wouldn't get anywhere else? Can you work with this person and still grow? Do you like the rest of the team? If you answered "yes" to most if not all of these questions, then at least put a time limit on your stay. Do you need to be at this company for more than a year to get where you want to in your career? Will your boss promote you after one year?

If you have resolved to stay and deal with this boss, then it is in your best interest to figure out what makes her tick. When you start really watching her, you will quickly pick up on the times to stay out of her way, ask for something, and toot your own horn. You might actually fall into a comfortable relationship once you are able to "read" her better.

confronting coworkers will not kill you

Most coworkers are not your friends, so throw out the notion of "hurting their feelings." This is business, so get it into your head that speaking up about an issue you are having with a coworker is seen as a sign of strength if delivered the right way. Chef Michelle Bernstein, owner of Michy's in South Beach, tells us that she confronts people daily, whether or not they work for her, are related to her, or are bigger than she is.

At one of my first restaurant jobs I was sexually confronted by a young punk. He was offended that I called him out on it and couldn't believe that I didn't back down when he stuck his nose in my face and put his hand in an inappropriate place. I screamed and told him exactly what I thought of him and what would become of him if he tried anything ever again. He quickly backed off and didn't bother me again. I believe that keeping things inside is like cancer, it makes you sick. So I deal with people directly and honestly. Always.

If you have a problem with someone, don't confront them in front of the group; it is disrespectful. Instead, pull them aside and share specific examples of your issues. Keep the emotion out of your voice, get your facts right, be willing to listen, and offer a solution to fix it from your end. Don't be condescending. Be willing to give a little, as in maybe you are partly responsible for the miscommunication.

However strongly we believe in confronting people who are causing you problems, there are types of coworkers who are worth resolving issues with and those who are not.

WORTH CONFRONTING

The credit-hogs

You can't just let someone take credit for your work, because if you let them get away with it a few times it will never stop.

The complainers

These are the ones who always have something negative to say. They just can't be positive about anything and eventually they will bring you and everyone else down.

The backstabbing phonies

These coworkers can undermine your credibility with just a few choice words to the right people. They are also often cowardly—that's why they are talking to others about you—so call them on their behavior and, believe us, they will zip it.

NEVER WORTH CONFRONTING

The crazies

We have all been there. The coworker who is just not right in the head. Stay away, you never know what will set her off and you don't want it to be you.

The woe is me's

These are the ones who are late because their car broke down, who sit at their desk crying for a week straight about the latest in a long line of breakups, who miss a deadline because they are distracted by the fight they had with their sister. You can be both frustrated by and sorry for these coworkers, but it isn't worth being part of their drama. Just know that soon enough your boss will be involved.

The impossibles

These are the colleagues who are notoriously difficult, the ones whom no one can stand. Better to bond with your team over your mutual dislike of this character because she is most likely on her way out the door. If no one can stand her, how do you think your boss feels?

taking ownership of success is scary

To say the sentence "I am successful" out loud is uncomfortable for most of us. There are several reasons why this is the case. As women, we have been raised to never boast, and downplaying our successes has become a comfortable way to connect with other people. Unfortunately, many of us are also still learning how to be happy for one another's success rather than just competitive. We are also learning how to support the choices made by other women and how to validate their individual definitions of success. Consider the ongoing tension between working and stay-at-home mothers. And despite all our other options, many of us just won't ever feel successful enough.

The key for all of us is to define our own success. Find happiness in what you spend the majority of your day doing and embrace what drives you. Your definition of success may also change throughout the years. Let yourself change and be willing to let your definition of professional success grow with you rather than dictate your goals.

our secret

If you are a believer in the Law of Attraction, positive thinking, or are a fan of "The Secret," then this will sound familiar. If you don't believe in any of those things and think that life just happens no matter what you put out into the world, then maybe we can change your thinking.

Girl's Guide was founded on our belief that women deserve to have their workplace issues addressed, that women can find strength in their differences, and that we all deserve to be in a profession that inspires us. Seems simple, right?

After a few setbacks when we gave into the naysayers, we did a lot of introspection. We reminded ourselves why we were juggling a public relations business during the day while staying up all night to write the books; taking red-eyes back from events so we could see our kids; and making time to help any woman with her career crises no matter how busy we found ourselves. We did and do all of this because we believe at our core that our message that women can be themselves in business and succeed is important enough to dedicate ourselves to.

We do have to share with you that during our negative days, life was exhausting. We felt burdened by everything that we had taken on, and unappreciated by the partners in our various projects. We commonly referred to Girl's Guide as "the rock" we just kept pushing up a very steep hill. But the truth is that being negative about your career is depleting. Complaining, griping, and criticizing can feel easier, but it really isn't. When you believe that you are surrounded by idiots and your boss just doesn't understand how hard you work and that you should work somewhere else but can't afford to leave your job—then you have accepted that your career is not under your control.

Professional happiness is absolutely within your control. And we know this because when we started thinking positively about the Girl's Guide message, amazing things began to happen. All of those rocks we were pushing started moving on their own. We were cast by Oxygen television to be career bloggers on their new Web site; our application to speak at a very exclusive conference was accepted; a hot production company signed us to develop a reality show that we had been thinking about for two years; we sold our third book and suddenly had the perfect idea for a fourth; and out of the blue came strangers who specialized in areas of business that we knew nothing about offering to help us.

Now you could say that it was pure coincidence. That we had

pushed those rocks so far that something had to actually manifest itself. But did our hard work really have to turn into something? There are enough failed businesses and unsold books out there for us to believe that our positive outlook affected this change. And frankly, feeling positive is energizing and worth a try. It can't hurt.

girl taking charge

We asked advertising executive Wendy Bengal if she had ever noticed confidence being a barrier to a woman's success. She told us this cautionary tale.

When I left a previous job, they chose a wonderful, bright woman for my replacement. She was soon calling me, frustrated because they had taken away some of her responsibility and not offered to let her touch other areas of the business. I pressed her, wondering if she'd simply asked why and made the case for her expertise. Her response was that she didn't want to appear to be questioning their judgment. "But you are questioning their judgment," I insisted. "And if you don't question it, they are going to start questioning the value of your position."

She thought of a million excuses why they made their decision (most were distorted assessments of herself) and why she should delay confronting them. Within a few months, my old boss called for recommendations on a replacement. After expressing her unhappiness with everyone except those who could address it, the woman chose to leave instead of promote her own value. When I spoke with her former boss about the skills the company had lost with her departure, I was floored by the response: "Wow. I wish I'd have known she could do that."

a view from the ladder

As principal/founder of The Castle Group, Inc., Sandy Lish has managed many women over the years. While she said people of both genders put up barriers to their own success, she does see things that tend to occur more with women. She shared with us some of the most common issues that she has noticed with her female employees.

Can you tell us some of the common career-stalling behaviors that you noticed among the women who work for you?
Women, especially young women, tend to make declarative statements that sound like questions because of the way their voices go up at the end. That sort of "Valley Girl" sound. This takes away from the statement and makes the speaker sound uncertain.

I have also noticed that women often use "little" as an adjective. Such as "Can you read this little memo I wrote?" Or "I'm getting a little award tonight at a little event." Is it a girl thing to be modest and try to minimize our successes? It shouldn't be—but sticking that "little" adjective in there downplays the importance of the noun that follows.

Even if it is trendy, dressing too provocatively, too casually, or in any way inappropriately minimizes your impact. People, and especially other women, notice what you have on and, right or wrong, form judgments that can stick. Please refrain from covering yourself in orange self-tanner, showing me your cleavage, or wearing flip-flops to my office if you want to make a solid first impression.

I have also had several women be too casual about how they present themselves professionally. I have interviewed women whose e-mail addresses were so cute that I immediately thought of them as unserious about their job search; one e-mail address actually began "lambchop@." This also holds true for overly casual voice mail greetings.

Are there barriers that fall along gender lines that can be transformed into positive attributes?

Absolutely there are, such as being sensitive to others (positive) vs. being too sensitive (negative!); being able to provide guidance (positive) vs. being able to hone in on others' flaws (negative!); being able to juggle multiple issues (positive) vs. being unable to say no (negative!); being a good role model for other working women and for your children (positive) vs. being conflicted about being a working mother (negative!).

six

[insert stereotype here]

Stereotypes are everywhere: women aren't just the fairer sex; we're the weaker and more emotional one too. We rant and rave and occasionally break down in tears. And for God's sake, don't talk to us when we're experiencing PMS. Women aren't strong leaders because they are too emotional. Women aren't strong leaders because they can't take charge. Women are not strong leaders because [insert stereotype here].

For real progress to occur, we have to improve our skills, market our accomplishments, mentor other women, and actively work to change the perceptions. Even the most enlightened among women fall trap to the stereotypes. A female senior executive in the pharmaceutical industry put it this way:

> I think women actually are more likely to react emotionally than men, perhaps because we tend to take criticism personally. And the

reality is that reacting emotionally does get in the way of collegial conversations about how to address a given problem. So I think the fact that women's emotions are viewed differently is actually rooted in the fact that we do react differently—we're more inclined to get upset. In an ideal world, women would have enough mentoring and coaching to ensure they have the confidence in themselves to help keep their defensive, emotional responses in check.

Girls, you've got to lead to succeed—even in entry-level positions. Perceptions won't change overnight, but that's no reason to let them keep you down. In this chapter we offer you stories and lessons that will show you how to use your emotional intelligence to your advantage.

the burden of the stereotype

Catalyst (those researchers again) analyzed numerous studies that have proven that men and women lead in very similar ways. Yet their 2005 report, *Women "Take Care," Men "Take Charge,"* showed that senior managers perceive sharp differences in leadership styles. And differences in perception lead to stereotypes—i.e., women are too emotional to be good leaders. These stereotypes not only undermine women's ability to lead but prevent us from getting the really big jobs—and really big paychecks.

The Catalyst survey asked male and female senior managers (CEOs and two levels below) to rate their perceptions of men and women in the ten key leadership behaviors: supporting, rewarding, mentoring, networking, consulting, team-building, inspiring, problem-solving, influencing upward, and delegating.

Both the men and women rated women as better at stereotypically feminine "caretaking skills" such as supporting and rewarding. And both sexes claimed that men excel at more conventionally masculine "taking charge" skills such as problem-solving and delegating responsibility.

Overall, the study found that women rated themselves higher than the men and that men saw women as superior in only two out of ten key leadership behaviors, supporting and rewarding subordinates. One caveat: men outnumbered women in the survey because men outnumber women in senior management.

The author of the study and director of research at Catalyst Jeanine Prime laid out the problem, "It is often these 'taking charge' skills—the stereotypically 'masculine' behaviors—that are seen as prerequisites for top-level positions."

For women in business, this is a real catch-22. Problem-solving, influencing superiors, delegating responsibility, and other "taking charge" skills are key components of what Catalyst's study terms "interpersonal power," which is the power of the individual—i.e., you inspire people around you to respond "you are a strong and charismatic leader; therefore I will follow you."

The study suggests that women, robbed of this interpersonal power, must rely more on "positional power," which is the power that comes with the job. As in "you are an executive vice president, therefore I will listen to you."

In effect it's a double-whammy—women aren't perceived of as having the "taking charge" skills *and* they make up only 16 percent of Fortune 500 corporate officers *and* in 2007 they made up less than 1 percent of the CEOs, so they don't have the power that comes with the job. Net-net: women don't have the power.

We need to change these perceptions, so we'll start with the stereotypes. We put the stereotypes to the test—a poll actually—and asked fifty women who work in a wide range of fields, at a wide range of levels, in a wide range of locations to answer a few questions about the most pervasive stereotypes about women's behavior in the workplace. We wanted to learn about crying, PMS, their perception of how women are perceived versus men, and if they are able to separate the professional from the personal.

Of the fifty women polled, thirty responded; enough to yield a representative sample, a few universal truths, and a number of interesting stories.

"there's no crying in baseball."

Oh yes there is. Every single respondent to our survey has cried at least once on the job and many a lot more than once. Ninety percent of the women blamed themselves for the breakdown. Whatever brought them to tears—and the most common reasons included the very valid reason of overwork, not enough support, and unfair criticism from superiors—was forgotten and overtaken by the shame and disappointment experienced because they lost their composure.

Even the most professionally tough women we know have broken down. An events director at an extremely high-profile restaurant in New York City whom we've worked with—and who's scared the bejesus out of us at every meeting with her dispassionate authoritative competence—described her experience, and it was echoed by many others: "It was 3 A.M. I was still at my desk trying to get more work done. I was tired and exhausted, physically and emotionally. I was more stressed and overworked than I have ever been. I felt that there was nothing else I could do to make it work. Nothing else I could do to make it better."

Karen Mellman-Smith, president of Spotlight Marketing, a firm that specializes in product integration in Chicago, tells of a crying experience that happened early in her career:

When I was at Kraft over fifteen years ago, I was working fourteen-hour days in a new products group and hadn't had a day off in months. My VP, who clearly had no regard or concern for my work-load and/or state-of-mind, dumped a whole other project *list* on my plate after I reviewed with her the ten thousand things I was already doing. I left her office, dropped my notes on my desk, headed for the bathroom, and cried my eyes out (which felt like a nervous breakdown at the time).

Similarly, an interior designer at an internationally famous design firm shared this crying story:

One of the first assignments at my new job was to design a hotel lobby, two retail concourses, and a new casino in a matter of days. I just didn't have enough time or experience and was at a complete loss. Everything that could go wrong went wrong, and things just got worse and worse. I stayed up for days, did all I could, but felt as if it would never come together. Covering my emotions has never been my forte, to say the least, so I just broke down and cried. Some people in my office probably still think I am mentally unstable.

From our perspective, none of these women sound mentally unstable—they just sound overworked, unsupported, and at the end of their rope. And when a woman gets to the end of her rope, she cries. It's not like we have so many other options. Marianne LaFrance, a psychology professor at Yale University, told the *New York Times*, "Men are allowed to be more direct. They can pound table tops and yell and throw something against walls and do various kinds of physical acting out. Women's mode of expression is supposed to be more passive, more childlike." She continued, "If women could act out like men, there would probably be less tears."

www.vault.com, a Web site that *Fortune* magazine called the "best place on the Web to prepare for a job search," wrote that "women and men are both emotional in their own ways, but the corporate world is much more attuned to, and accepting of, traditional male emotional response (arguing, back-slapping, yelling) than female emotional response (hugging, crying, self-deprecation). If you're a woman, try to cut back on classic female emotional responses."

And the boys aren't the only ones trying to get us to keep those tears at bay. In the short-lived *The Apprentice: Martha Stewart*, which aired in 2005, Martha made international news when she delivered, through her perennially clenched jaw, the line heard round the world, "Cry, you're out of here. Women in business don't cry, my dear."

Women do cry and it's not a weakness of spirit or just their nature. It's *actually* nature. Check out the science:

- Men's and women's tear glands are structurally different, causing women's tears to pour down their face while men's tears just brim at the lower eyelids (so you may not even know if a man is crying);
- Before puberty, boys and girls cry the same amount, but by age eighteen, women cry substantially more;
- The proteins released in emotional tears (versus the ones that stream down your face in the wind, ruining your makeup before you've even started the day) are the same ones found in hormones associated with high stress, including prolactin and adrenocorticotropic hormone;
- Women have nearly double the prolactin levels of men, whose levels decline sharply after puberty.

And this is just the science. What about socialization? Boys don't cry. We all know it and teach our sons, too. As a matter of fact, men cry so rarely (women cry four times more) that a study done by Pennsylvania State University found evidence that men's tears are viewed more positively than women's. "It seems that because men are less frequently noticed crying, they're given the benefit of the doubt," said Stephanie Shields, a professor of psychology and women's studies, who led the study—while women, if you're to believe Martha, should be fired.

girl taking charge: caitlin cried. once.

When I worked as an assistant producer in television, I was managed by a very volatile woman who entrusted me with enormous amounts of responsibility without training or even asking if I knew what I was doing. If I'd had a background in television production or any confidence in my knowledge of the industry, I would have viewed her absentee management as an opportunity to move quickly up through the ranks. But as I came from a different industry and had no experience, I needed a lot more support. I hadn't even written a script before I started the job, and she knew it when she hired me. I had energy, passion, intelligence, contacts, a great work ethic, and a desire to learn, but no practical experience. For me to succeed, I needed a manager who would guide me every step of the way—for a very short time—until I learned the ropes. She was not this type of manager, not by a long shot— and left me completely on my own. About three months into my tenure, my absentee boss was on location on a shoot. She called me from the location looking for some footage that had yet to arrive. I took the call in a public room where I was surrounded by colleagues. My manager wanted to know where the boxes were. She didn't ask me to track the packages, oh no, she screamed at me repeatedly like a maniac and told me I was doing a terrible job, and couldn't believe that *I was doing this to her*, that the shoot was ruined. On and on and on, she screamed. It went on for so long, and my face got so red, that a few of my colleagues came over and patted me on the shoulder in support. After she hung up on me because the FedEx driver arrived with the boxes during the call, I started crying. And when I start crying, I find it very difficult to stop. I was humiliated. I had let a complete idiot get the best of me. I let her scream at me and, even worse, I stayed at the job instead of walking out. I was gone less than six months after that. And that was the first and last time I cried at work. I had a revelation: if it is bad enough to make me cry, then it isn't a place I want to be.

Since we can't physically stop crying when we're pushed to the brink, we need to find ways to stay away from the brink and change the perception about crying in the workplace. Here's a place to start:

1. Support the sisterhood. If you see a colleague, subordinate, or manager crying, be sympathetic. Give her some privacy, or help her get to a private spot to cry it out. Once she's finished crying, see if you can help her figure out what brought on the tears. If the reasons are professional, offer some solutions to her problems. If she is on your team, it is absolutely essential that you support her not just with sympathetic words but with action in the form of more resources, training, or access to you.

2. Cry in private. The fewer people who see you cry, the better. Try to bite your lip or take deep breaths until you can make it to the ladies room or, better yet, outside the building.

3. Enact a zero tolerance policy for abusive, demeaning, or rude behavior and make sure everyone in the organization is on board. One professional writer tells of the time in her first job when she was reduced to tears not because she made a huge mistake that was printed in the magazine (which she did feel terrible about) but rather because of the reaction by her male manager. Instead of working with her to make sure she had the training and support to ensure that mistakes wouldn't happen again, he gave her a lecture on what a disappointment she was to him and to *everyone* who had recommended her to him for the job.

"it must be her time of the month."

According to www.womenshealthchannel.com, "Women may experience emotional and physical changes prior to menstruation. The medical term for these changes is 'premenstrual syndrome,' commonly called PMS. More than 150 symptoms are associated with PMS, ranging from breast tenderness to nausea to anger and irritability."

Because there is no diagnostic test for PMS and because there are so many symptoms that are largely self-reported, exact numbers of women afflicted with PMS are difficult to determine, but ranges do exist. According to a study published in *Practical Strategies in Obstetrics and Gynecology* in 2000, an estimated 75 percent to 90 percent (somewhere between 43 and 55 million, using U.S. Census Bureau data) of reproductive-age women in the United States experience some adverse symptoms during the premenstrual phase of their cycle. Of these women, approximately 20 percent to 40 percent (or 12 to 25 million) believe they have symptoms bothersome enough to qualify as premenstrual syndrome (PMS). Approximately 3 percent to 8 percent (2 to 5 million) of these women have symptoms that are severe enough to meet the criteria for premenstrual dysphoric disorder (PMDD).

The symptoms vary from woman to woman and from cycle to cycle. Their intensity ranges from mild to incapacitating, and even though it's not exactly clear what *causes* premenstrual syndrome, a combination of physiological, genetic, nutritional, and behavioral factors are likely involved.

What about our sample? Of the thirty respondents, 66 percent or twenty of our girls reported symptoms of PMS, one had been diagnosed with and was being treated for PMDD, and nine reported no symptoms, although one of them described herself as "moody all the time."

So PMS exists and a bunch of us suffer from it each and every month. Not a news flash. The real issue is whether or not PMS affects our productivity. Unfortunately, reliable studies don't exist. All of the data in these studies is self-reported—meaning the studies simply ask women if PMS affects their ability to do work. And according to our group, PMS absolutely does *not* affect our performance on the job.

The only good thing about PMS is that you know it's coming, so you can plan for it. Don't be like Kim and take fifteen years to figure out that PMS is the reason she hates her husband the same day every month (she thought *he* was the jerk!). PMS is the one time where you can confidently say, "I'm the problem." So minimize the problem. Whenever possible, don't schedule important meetings during PMS and always take a minute after a situation annoys you to ask yourself if it were any other time of the month, would you react the same way? PMS is not an excuse, it's a fact of life and we can all manage it with a little planning. However, don't mess around with severe PMS—if you are experiencing migraines, depression, or severe mood swings, you could be suffering from PMDD and should see a doctor as soon as possible.

"when men raise their voices, they are expressing passionate opinions. when women raise their voices, they are hysterical."

Sometimes life just ain't fair and this is one of those times. Men are perceived differently in the workplace and they have more advantages. Numerous studies support it. Our poll supports it. Even www.askmen.com supports it. ". . . because men don't give [women] the proper respect in the first place. If men treated [women] as equal associates, then you would not be reading about this topic in this column. The unfortunate truth is that discrimination at the workplace exists, even if the situation has improved and progress is being made."

Every woman in the workplace knows that men get a free pass when it comes to expressing emotions. So what can we do about it? First, stereotypes are more easily believed about people we don't know—so advocate for the people you do know. If you manage a team of women, then have a meeting to address the challenges women face in the workplace. Educate them about the perceived differences in men's behavior and create a system for calling the team out when they fall back on stereotypes—whether they are acting in ways that support the stereotypes or attributing someone else's behavior to the stereotypes.

If you are a new employee and not sure what the company ethos is, then bring up the subject and try to get a dialogue going in a positive way. One easy way is to call attention to an article you were reading in a newspaper or trade journal about the subject and have a discussion with the group about it. Better yet, bring this book into work and use it as a catalyst for conversation. Even the busiest managers welcome a constructive suggestion. Broach the subject at an appropriate time and be positive. These can be sensitive issues to discuss, so be savvy about the politics. If you're feeling nervous, then give a quick read to the office politics chapter later on in the book before you attempt a dialogue.

And if a man is raising his voice, ask him why he's getting so emotional. Watch how quickly he shuts up.

"it's just business. don't take it personally."

The overwhelming majority of our respondents felt badly when a manager made this statement to them. Most felt "demeaned" and "devalued." However, when pressed, they would admit that this statement does help put things in perspective and help set priorities. Work is important, and it's important to do a good job to make a good living to support yourself and your family. Therefore, it's extremely difficult not to take our work personally. Most of us spend more time working than we do with our families. We invest our energy, creativity, and self-esteem in the work that we do and when things go wrong (and they always do) it hurts.

It helps, as the phrase suggests, to try to keep things in perspective. An assistant to a very high profile chef and restaurateur told us, "I am emotionally involved in my work, but over the years I think I've learned to let go at some level. I get paid well, but I don't get paid enough to worry at the owners' level. If I'm stressing out and the owners aren't, then I can let go of that issue. Yoga definitely helps calm the mind!!"

When Andrea Rosen, vice president of special markets at HarperCollins, is told, "it's just business, don't take it personally," she accepts it as a positive reminder. "It makes me realize that life and work are in balance, and you can be passionate about your job and want to succeed but don't need to be overly emotional about it."

Liz Morrow, a media buyer who has recently started her own business so she can spend more time with her family, puts it this way, "At the end of the day, I go home to three great kids and a great husband. That puts 'business' into perspective. I love my job, I love the people I work with, but at the end of the day, it is all about my home. Not about business."

And yet some situations in the workplace do feel personal and you have to find a way to deal with them. A food stylist in New York shared her experience: "A male coworker was deeply offended by something I had done despite assurances that it had nothing to do with him. It was partly a union issue and partly personal and he believed that it was intentionally done in secret from him. He responded by refusing to speak to me, or acknowledge my presence during the workday. We had previously had a close and very amiable work relationship. He would literally turn his back on me when I greeted him. Not only was it an unprofessional response, I was also personally offended that he would choose to take this course rather than try to work it out with me. For a while, I chose to let him have his 'thing,' thinking it would play out, employing the 'it's just business' point of view. But eventually, it became difficult to work well, in both a practical and emotional way. It wasn't worth it to me to remain silent, as it was destroying my enjoyment of my work environment. I initiated a discussion, during which I apologized for unintentionally offending him, which resulted in restoring our working relationship. However, my personal feelings toward this person suffered, and I now maintain a subtle distance from him. But that I can live with, it's just business."

QUIZ: CAN YOU COPE?

Work is stressful. Do you have what it takes to stay calm when the pressure mounts? Everybody is exposed to stressful situations, both positive and negative. Stress is an integral element in the lives of all creatures, and it plays an important role in survival. Nevertheless, stress can have negative effects on our physical and emotional health.

What matters though is not the number of stressful situations that we are exposed to or the amount of stress that we have to withstand. Once again, it's our perception of the stressor, and how we react to it. When you're overworked and overtired, you're coping skills will be depleted.

Ask yourself these questions. If you answer more yeses than nos, then your coping skills need work.

- Are you easily discouraged when things don't go your way?
- Do you feel overwhelmed when you have too many things to do?

- Do you respond to professional criticism as a personal attack?
- Do you lose your temper when things go wrong?
- Do you regularly raise your voice?
- Have you noticed people behaving differently with you in comparison to their other colleagues?
- Is crying in response to a situation the rule rather than the exception?

"she has kids so she . . ."

People assume many things about working mothers. Some of them are true (we are tired, a lot of the time) and some are not (all of us would rather be home), but be aware when you return to work after having a baby that they exist. We have outlined a few of the most common stereotypes below.

AFTER BECOMING A PARENT, SHE LOST HER EDGE

This is a stereotype that drives us insane. Just because we have become mothers does not mean we have been sapped of our ambition. Our priorities may have changed a bit (OK, a lot), but that doesn't mean that we can't be a strong, powerful asset to any company.

WORKING MOMS WOULD RATHER BE HOME WITH THEIR CHILDREN

This one drives us crazy too. Not all of us fantasize about being a stay-at-home mom. That doesn't mean we don't absolutely adore our children, it just means that some of us like more of a balance between working and mothering. Because many people assume that you are not returning from maternity leave, or when back at work you resent being there, or worse that you are planning your escape route, it can be very hard to get back into the swing of things. But if none of that is true, then your hard work and focus will turn them around. You will always be walking a fine line, however, because you don't want to sacrifice your work/life balance just because of some stereotype.

WOMEN WITH FAMILIES ARE UNWILLING TO RELOCATE FOR THEIR BUSINESS

Unfair! Some of us would jump at the chance to try something new, and some of us have families who would be excited and supportive of that opportunity. Check in with your family to see how they would feel about a relocation. If everyone would be up for it, then make it quite clear to your boss that you are throwing your hat in the ring.

WORKING MOMS WILL FOREVER BE LEAVING EARLY, STAYING HOME WITH SICK KIDS, OR RUNNING OFF TO SCHOOL PLAYS

When you are planning a family, you also must plan for how to care for the family if you have work responsibilities. It's the part that most of us leave out when trying to get pregnant. It's only after the baby has arrived and you are looking at only a month left of maternity leave that it hits you . . . what if the baby gets sick and can't go to day care? What if my partner is unable to pick the baby up when I am out of town on business? What if my child joins a soccer league and I have weekend workshops scheduled? It's smart to think about all of the issues that may come up (or at least a good portion of them) and how you are going to handle them, because even the most family friendly organization is going to become impatient if you are never around because you are too busy attending to your family.

R-E-S-P-E-C-T: GIRLS ON TV SMASHING STEREOTYPES

Watching movies is one of our favorite ways to relax, so we always include a movie list in our books that feature women in the workplace. Since we're not too proud to admit that we love television too, *The Girl's Guide to Kicking Your Career into Gear* presents our list of top ten television shows that feature strong powerful women, being themselves and being treated as equals. Too bad most of our girls star in science fiction or fantasy shows. We've still got a long way to go, but with a nod to the girls who started it all, Mary Tyler Moore and Marlo Thomas, this list should provide hours of enjoyment and inspiration.

1. ***That Girl*** Marlo Thomas started it all back in the sixties when she starred as one of television's first leading ladies who was an independent and single woman. Each week, as the wanna-be Broadway actress Ann Marie, Marlo would confront the heartaches and joys of living in Manhattan. We love her attitude, apartment, relationship with her boyfriend Donald, and of course her clothes.

2. ***The Mary Tyler Moore Show*** Watch Mary gain confidence through the years in the newsroom. She deals with a difficult boss and nutty colleagues. She's got great friends and a series of terrible dates. And we definitely don't love the clothes—those seventies pants suits—eek.

3. ***Grey's Anatomy*** We're guessing *Grey's* is so good because it's written and executive-produced by a woman— Shonda Rhimes. She manages to pack all the challenges that women face in the workplace into each week. The women doctors and interns overcome their struggles by leaning on each other.

4. ***Gilmore Girls*** Lorelai Gilmore is one of the cool modern

women on television. The show manages to champion Lorelai's single motherhood while showcasing all the sacrifices and challenges that she had to make for choosing this path.

5. *Veronica Mars* Cancelled prematurely because of low ratings, this critical darling was one of the best shows on television. Really, check out the three seasons on DVD and you will see what we are talking about. High school private eye Veronica Mars, as played by the amazing Kristen Bell, is the type of female character we love—smart, loyal, and brimming with major attitude.

6. *Battlestar Galactica* The Top Guns are women pilots. The president is a woman who was formerly a school-teacher. The bathrooms are coed. Equality reigns in this future land. Of course, it doesn't hurt that all of the guys are hot and there's lots of romance and sex.

7. *Buffy the Vampire Slayer* We'd always been a bit sheepish about admitting just how much fun and empowering it was to watch a girl kick vampire ass. Not until we watched the DVDs' extras (another embarrassing admission!) were we validated for loving Buffy. The creator (a man) and the writers (men and women) committed to creating a character that was strong, likeable, and beautiful who also happened to be a demon-killer destined to save the world.

8. *Xena: Warrior Princess* Not just for lesbians, we swear. Our guilty pleasure on Saturday mornings in the 1990s. Xena, a mighty warrior and healer played by the flawless Lucy Lawless (she pops up in *Battlestar Galactica*, too), once led a band of outlaws who terrorized all of ancient Greece. She regrets the harm she caused and, with companion and bard Gabrielle by her side, she travels the countryside fighting the forces of evil and atoning for the sins of her past.

9. *The X Files* follows the adventures and lives of FBI agents Fox Mulder, the believer, and Dana Scully, the

skeptic, as they investigate cases that involve the paranormal or previously unsolved (especially by conventional means) activity.

10. ***Alias*** Sydney Bristow is a young, athletic college graduate who was recruited in her freshman year as a secret agent for SD-6, a top-secret branch of the CIA. When Sydney confides her lifestyle to her boyfriend, the head of SD-6 has him killed and Sydney learns that SD-6 is part of a rogue agency out to rule the world. She becomes a double agent, working with the real CIA to bring down SD-6 with the help of her handler, Michael Vaughn (hello, Michael Vartan), and her estranged, double agent father. Along the way, Sydney fights various rival agents, rival terrorist groups, and traitors all the while keeping her secret from her friends.

a view from the ladder

Stephanie Shields, a professor of psychology and women's studies and Ph.D. from Pennsylvania State University, has spent the better part of twenty years talking to women about gender and emotion. Her book, *Speaking from the Heart: Gender and the Social Meaning of Emotion (Studies in Emotion and Social Interaction)* (Cambridge University Press; June 2002) uses examples from everyday life, contemporary culture, and the latest research to illustrate how culturally shared beliefs about emotion are used to shape our identities as women and men. Everything from nineteenth-century ideals of womanhood to baseball and the new man is considered in the context of how emotion affects our everyday lives. She recently became interested in women, work, and emotion, most especially the politics of emotion in the workplace, work-family emotional pressures on women, and emotion regulation because these issues come up in nearly every conversation she has with women. Stephanie's work not only validates what we all feel but also offers us some strategies for shifting perceptions and ultimately overriding stereotypes.

So we're not paranoid? Your research has actually proven that women's and men's emotions are perceived differently in the workplace. Can you tell us about that?

Men get the benefit of the doubt. Our work has shown that if a man is emotional, it's assumed that he's got a darn good reason. Part of the problem with even talking about emotion is the fundamental double bind that women face: if we show emotions in the workplace, then we're "too emotional," and it's assumed that we are unable to control ourselves and act rationally. If we don't show emotion, however, then we're judged to be cold and inhuman—especially if the "missing emotions" are care and concern.

Doing this work for the past twenty years has helped me tune in to women's stories. One topic that women will and can start a conversation anywhere about is ways in which they've had to struggle to manage their emotions or how the emotions of other people have gotten in the way of their progress.

When are we too emotional?

What does that really mean? Let's think about what "emotional" might mean. Do women experience emotion more intensely than men? Express it more easily? Have more positive emotion? More negative emotion? Experience a wider range of emotions? What research shows is simply that (in the United States) women are more expressive generally—that is, we tend to show more variation in expression and voice than men on average, and perhaps more significantly, women are just more willing to talk about emotion.

In fact, when men express emotion it may not be recognized or labeled as "emotion." When I began to investigate the stereotype of "masculine inexpression," I realized that there are a number of areas of behavior that are quite identified with masculinity—like competitive sports—where emotion is totally appropriate, but that we never think of as "emotional" in quite the same way as emotion associated with women. Do you remember *Wide World of Sports* on ABC? The program's motto was "the thrill of victory and the agony of defeat." Do the words thrill and agony not connote emotion? Competitive sports are filled with the full range of emotions: euphoria in winning, dismay and anger at losing. It is impossible to watch a game, any game, without seeing lots of emotion expressed, sometimes even crying. Yet when we think about competitive sports, we never think about how emotional they are—even though they are saturated with emotion.

When men and women display the same behaviors, yelling and crying, they are perceived in a completely different way. As a matter of fact, white men even get a little boost when they are labeled emotional. "Wow, if he's emotional, it must be important." With women, though, you're damned if you do and damned if you don't.

What about crying?
Tears are really amazing in that they are an emotional expression that occurs when we've exhausted every other means available to handle a situation. Genuine tears are about as real as you get when you experience deeply felt emotions. Tears come when you feel disempowered to fix the situation. The sad thing is that people are skeptical of women's tears. Women are perceived to have more control over their tears, which leads to suspicion. "Is she really crying because she's hurt or because she wants to manipulate a situation?"

It is hard to control tears, but they are a little less likely to happen if we understand the situations that trigger them. Try to recognize the circumstances under which you cry. Quite often you will see that it's a situation that you feel is wrong, that is important to you, but that you feel that you have no way to fix or even to say exactly what needs fixing. If you really try to understand what it is about the situation that you feel helpless against, you'll be less caught up in the tears themselves. Figure out what is taxing your coping resources and what you need so you can cope again. Sometimes it's simply an arrogant and dictatorial boss, and recognizing this will help you better evaluate your options, even if the only one is to look for another job.

How do we make it better?

Emotion isn't particularly easy to control—if it were, we wouldn't be having this conversation! Still, there are some strategies that help. One of the easiest and most effective to use is to recognize the power of "emotional language." Be careful not to label yourself "emotional," and don't let others label you as "emotional."

Never use emotional language against yourself. Stop yourself from falling into the trap of going along with the stereotype of the "too emotional" woman. Do not say things like, "I am so overwhelmed and can't deal." It may be how you're feeling at that moment, but most of the women I've met cope with things pretty darn well and don't need to undermine their achievements. If you call yourself "overwhelmed," I guarantee that everyone who hears you will, without thinking, put you in the category of a "too emotional female"—that's not what you want or deserve.

Recognize that when someone labels you as "emotional," it undermines your credibility. When someone accuses you of getting emotional about an issue, don't take the bait by arguing (emotionally) and responding "I am not!!" Turn it around! Patiently explain that actually you're addressing a significant issue. Don't they think it's worth investing some energy in it? How can they argue?

change is often good

Fear of change is one of the biggest barriers to success that women face. Fear of change will cause us to stay in a safe job instead of moving on. Yet changes come no matter how hard we try to avoid them, so in this chapter we get you prepared for some of your career's potentially biggest challenges, including getting fired and identifying when you need to make a change. This chapter will explore changes big and small and show you how to make the most of them.

ARGUMENT AGAINST TAKING A JOB JUST FOR THE MONEY

Here is a story to remind you that you need to keep thinking about your career in the big picture.

Jessica was kicking ass as a retail manager in Florida. She was promoted several times over the course of two years, and at the very young age of twenty-three she was managing her own team. The corporation took notice and offered her a big salary increase if she would move to New York City. Having dreamed of Manhattan since a family trip when she was twelve, she jumped at the chance. And it sounded like so much money.

When she arrived at her new store, she realized that turning it around was a big job. Three months in and she was working sixteen hours a day, seven days a week. A year in and the hours weren't diminishing. She hadn't even had the time to visit the Empire State Building. And the salary, which would have bought a nice house in Miami, barely covered a shared apartment in Queens. But she had an epiphany while training with the executives at the corporation and saw that their schedules weren't any better. Sure, down the road she may be driving a Lexus rather than a Subaru, but she wouldn't have a moment with her family if she ever even found the time to fall in love and get married. In fact, other than grabbing an occasional beer with a coworker, she hadn't had time to develop new friendships outside of work.

On her twenty-fifth birthday she decided to quit the company and move home without another job. Within her first week back, she landed a sales job, reconnected with her friends, and signed up to learn a new language. She found that time was a more important asset to her than money.

it may be time to look

Putting your head in the sand is never a good idea. When you aren't paying attention to what is going on around you or right in front of you, then you are missing your career guideposts. Those are the signs that are telling you to leave, change, or try to save your job. We have offered you a few signs that something is shifting in your professional world and it may be time to take action.

There is a high probability that you will soon be shown the door if:

- Your boss isn't looking you in the eye;
- You are no longer invited to key meetings;
- You are kept out of the loop;
- Suddenly there is no pressure on you from above to meet deadlines; and
- Your boss is suddenly vague about your involvement in future projects.

It looks likely that your boss is going to be quitting if she:

- Is unengaged in meetings and projects;
- Is either tense (afraid of being fired) or too relaxed (preparing to quit);
- Has gone from focused and clear to completely distracted;
- Spends more time out for vague appointments; and
- Has no sense of urgency about anything.

Your company may be closing its doors or going through a big change if:

- There is a general air of anxiety among senior employees;
- Closed door meetings suddenly become the norm; and
- You encounter several hushed discussions among key staff.

being fired just may be the best thing that's ever happened

If you are fired or laid off, you can expect that you are going to mourn the loss in some way. If you loved the job, then this can be a really tough process, but even if you didn't, don't underestimate the emotional impact that losing a job can have on your self-esteem.

Grief is what we feel after any major loss and no matter how we felt about our work, firing or a layoff falls under that description. Dr. Elisabeth Kübler-Ross named the five stages of grief that most of us go through after a loss. We asked Diana, a woman we interviewed who had been laid off from her job as a vice president of development for a major network, to take us through her post-firing grieving process. Diana had poured her heart into the job and weathered new bosses, slashed budgets, and a job title that didn't change even after she asked and asked. When she was unceremoniously booted— on the heels of a big success she had orchestrated for the network— she was shocked. Here's how it hit her.

DENIAL

"This was definitely where I was at first. I couldn't believe that I was hearing what I was hearing. *They* were letting *me* go? Sure, I had thought about leaving, but it never occurred to me that it would be their choice. I just shut down. For about a week actually."

When your mind is processing anything big like this, you need time to adjust. During the denial stage, even if you feel like you are shutting down, you are actually wrapping your head around what has happened.

ANGER

"I'm not sure this is a stage that I will ever get 100 percent past, but in the beginning I was beyond angry. I was furious. I hated everything having to do with the network from the obvious (my boss) to the random (their logo)."

Sure, be furious, hate everyone—especially your ex-boss. Vent to your friends about everything having to do with your former company. But don't hold onto that anger without using it to motivate you. Unfortunately, many people can't get past this stage in part because it is easier to be angry about a firing than to be depressed about it. Anger is also the go-to emotion when we're embarrassed.

BARGAINING

"I had this ongoing interior dialogue about the fact that I was fired. I would promise myself that I would never let it happen again, that it was their fault not mine, that next time I would quit first."

During this stage we are trying to take control by making deals with ourselves. It is perfectly natural to want to do everything possible to avoid a situation like this ever happening again, but be realistic about the fact that even if you were the best employee in the world, you still could be fired.

DEPRESSION

"Oh, I was there. Lying on my bed in a darkened room. Staring at the ceiling and reliving that moment when my boss said 'it just isn't working.' It was really hard for me to find the energy to update my résumé, never mind network. I felt humiliated, so I didn't want to have to tell people what happened."

A dangerous stage for anyone is to stay in too long after a job loss. The fact is that the faster you refocus your energy on finding a new situation for yourself, the better. If you get into the mind-set that this is an opportunity for you to figure out what you really want from your professional life, you can take advantage of this huge upheaval. If the job and company were a right fit for you, then you most likely would still be there, right? So something wasn't working, and maybe it was something totally out of your control, like the financial stability of the organization. Be sad about the loss of the job but don't sink into a depression over it. *No job* is worth your mental health.

ACCEPTANCE

"It took me a while to get here, but I did. I went through a lot of ups and downs over the past five months but am so much happier than I ever thought I would be. After many interviews, I finally decided to open my own business, which has been scary but so much better than working for someone else."

Being laid off or fired defines you only if you let it. You just don't know what is waiting for you if you accept what has happened and start looking ahead of you instead of behind.

girl taking charge

Following a heartbreaking layoff at her dream job, Cori Snyder, a former marketing executive, eventually found herself with an unexpected new career. We spoke to her about the roller-coaster ride that led her to discovering a new professional self, an inventor of a board game for foodies called Celebrity Chef!

You were laid off a few years ago . . .
Yes, I was let go from what I had considered my dream job. The company was going through some cost cutting, and therefore eliminated a handful of positions in a series of rolling cuts. I had been there only a year, which made it especially painful, as I felt like I had only just gotten there.

You are now busy launching a brand-new concept for a board game. In retrospect, was being laid off a good thing?
That's a tough one. I loved my job, and think I could have been happy there and could have made a significant contribution to the company. And while these days it is almost de rigueur to be laid off at least once in your career, it is still very difficult, especially when it is in a company where layoffs come in ones, twos, and threes as opposed to the hundreds, and it feels that much more personal.

What did you go through emotionally following the layoff?
Given that I had considered it the perfect place for me, it really spurred some intense soul searching about what to do next. Our

identities are so connected with what we do for a living that not working—and not knowing how and where to move forward—really affects the psyche.

How did you arrive at being an entrepreneur?
As I went through the job search process without being excited by much of anything out there, I kept coming back to my desire to start my own business and finally decided that the time was right, and that I should "take advantage" of being let go.

Are you happy with that decision?
While my new venture is still in the beginning stages, I am thrilled and am the happiest professionally that I have been since my early twenties, a time when I started my own nonprofit organization. I have had many business ideas over the years but was too scared to leave the safety and security of a full-time job to do anything about them. My involuntary unemployment—in my mind a sort of hitting bottom, with no job and no income—made me less afraid of taking a risk, and made me see that I should take control of my career instead of continuing at the mercy of others.

a view from [jumping off] the ladder

Tiscia Eicher, a former corporate executive, describes herself as "pretty risk averse." The moves she's made in her life and career have all been carefully thought out and extensively researched. She doesn't make quick decisions and she doesn't make big changes. Until now. After twenty years in the workforce, Tiscia has decided to quit her job and take a year off to relax and put down some roots.

Tiscia graduated from Cornell University and immediately set to work in the hospitality industry in restaurant operations. She loved the business but didn't love working the nights, weekends, and holidays that the industry required. Deciding that an M.B.A. would be the logical next step, Tiscia applied and was accepted to the prestigious Kellogg School of Management at Northwestern University in Evanston, Illinois. She enrolled in the marketing program and fell in love with the craft. She graduated from Kellogg and moved to New York to join American Express to market the card to the restaurant and hospitality industry—merging her two passions.

Tiscia loved American Express and was fortunate to work with a number of incredible bosses and leaders. After a few years in New York, she wanted to move back to Chicago and began championing her desire through the halls of AmEx. When a job came up in the Chicago office to run the regional marketing division, Tiscia got her wish and worked for AmEx for another eight years, traveling extensively all the while.

Meanwhile, one of her friends from Cornell had become the president of the Calphalon corporation. When they were opening their first-ever culinary center in Chicago, she called Tiscia to get her ideas for the new center and recruiting good staff in her hometown. Inevitably, Calphalon hired Tiscia to run the two corporate culinary centers. After Tiscia joined the company, she helped establish and define the need for a dedicated brand-marketing department—and took on the task of developing that department six months after she started.

Although Tiscia was able to maintain her home base of operations in Chicago, the job required frequent trips to Toledo and Atlanta and she was rarely home. And although at Calphalon she became a vice president and part of the executive team, she drifted farther away not only from her love of brand marketing but also from her beloved city that she worked so hard to get back to. Tiscia made a bold move and asked to step down off the executive committee and become a director of marketing, where she could have a more direct hand in the programs she wanted to implement. She hired and trained a team, and the company has continued to grow and increase sales during her tenure.

After an extremely successful run with Calphalon, it became

time for her to try something new and close to home. Traveling for the better part of fifteen years takes a toll—and not just physically. Tiscia found it challenging to find time for herself. She found herself spending every weekend doing chores that piled up while she was gone and getting ready for the trip the following week. And while she loved the benefits of a large corporation and the team she built, the reality of her job was travel and meetings. She's now looking for a job that will be low on travel and high on creativity.

We spoke to Tiscia on her last day in corporate life for a while. She's decided to take a year off to relax and explore some new options—the first of which being her hometown.

Ever the resourceful girl, even in major life changes, Tiscia shares her thoughts in her "Five Things You Need to Do to Make a Big Life Change."

1. **Plan for it financially.** If you can live a little beneath your means, meaning don't spend every cent you make, you can start saving money in an effective and meaningful way. If you plan ahead and create some discipline early on, you create the latitude to have many options down the road.

2. **Don't plan too much.** I intend to take this year and explore as many options as I can for myself. I know I love marketing and plan to be working again after a year, however I am not exactly sure what that's going to look like—and that's okay. I am considering teaching, marketing a nonprofit, or maybe doing something completely different. I am going to let it play out.

3. **Identify what's important to you and go for it.** I have loved my career for the last twenty years, but the amount of travel I did never let me put down roots. I always wanted a dog and now I am going to get one. I am going to see my friends more, and I am going to take tennis lessons. They aren't huge things, but important ones that I haven't been able to get to while commuting between Chicago, Toledo, and Atlanta.

4. **Enlist some support.** Big changes are scary—especially for someone like me, who always chooses the conservative path. I am really lucky in that I have my sister as a role model. She actually retired at forty-three, and has supported my decision to take a year off and helped me plan for it too. I don't know if I would have done it without her advice.

5. **Trust yourself.** I know quitting my job and taking a year off is the right move for me, and I am going to make the most of it. Don't ignore what your gut is telling you to do.

PART FOUR

think big

running for (the corner) office

Research carried out by Roffey Park, a UK-based executive education and research organization, suggests that "managers have had to become far more adept at influencing, negotiating and navigating organizations—playing politics" in order to get things done. The same study suggests that the only way to get ahead is to spend far more time influencing and networking than would have been the case a decade ago. Their "Management Agenda 2007" survey found that office politics ranks as the highest cause of professional stress, even above issues of increased workload and problems with management. The survey of almost five hundred managers also revealed that conflict in the workplace is on the rise, with four out of ten attributing office politics as the main cause of this increase.

Yikes! Can this be true? Has the workplace regressed to high school, with cliques and backstabbing, boyfriend stealing, and gossip? Well, we hope not boyfriend stealing, but the other behaviors are certainly in evidence. In *The Girl's Guide to Being the Boss (without being a bitch)* we gave you all the lessons to rise above the politics (and we'll share some of those lessons here, too). But for a girl to really succeed in her career, she has to not only rise above the politics, she has to master the game. This chapter will show you how to play politics like the big boys—but only long enough to win, so that as women in power, you can change the rules. Don't hate the player, hate the game.

how to play

One of our favorite girls learned her lesson about office politics the hard way. When she was a young writer, she got a staff writing job for a magazine. It was the dream gig: she got to write about what she loved and work from her home in New York while the magazine was based in Texas. She worked extremely hard to develop sources within the industries she covered and eventually won people over by her work ethic and smarts. She never missed a deadline and she gained the respect of her peers—yet she was not a valued employee, received mediocre reviews, and had her fair share of uncomfortable conversations with management. She found out later that her editors spoke negatively of her and during her tenure they frequently changed her copy without her approval and/or knowledge.

Only with hindsight did she see what went wrong: she didn't play politics. A pretty straightforward girl in all of her communication, when asked a question, she'd answer quickly and from the heart, never considering what the person on the other end of the phone or e-mail might have wanted to hear. Without the benefit of "face time" with her colleagues, she couldn't develop positive relationships and therefore didn't earn the benefit of the doubt. She never saw her management's interaction with others or dropped by their desks for a casual chat. Picking up on politics is challenging for any new person, and doubly hard when you're not in the office. Don't make her mistake and realize it only after it's too late.

read the room

Don't be naive and think you can be above politics. Whether you engage in them or not, they're happening, so you've got to be prepared. When you're new to a group, even if you're the leader, it's important to pay attention to the culture in place. How do people communicate with one another? In person? On the phone? Via e-mail? Do they have formal meetings or informal ones? Do people challenge other people's ideas in public? Or keep their comments to themselves? When you first arrive at a new workplace, do more listening than talking for as long as possible. See if people in the organization are blogging—you may pick up some clues there.

The easiest way to get off on the wrong foot is to inadvertently offend the new group. Take your cues from your supervisor and act accordingly. Be very aware of cultural differences, especially if you've recently relocated. Occasionally you'll get lucky and figure out the politics straightaway, though more commonly it will take a few months.

If you notice a negative culture, and you're not in a leadership position with the power to change it, then start looking for another job. Immediately.

be careful whom you trust

At one of Kim's first jobs in publishing, she thought everyone liked her. She generated fantastic publicity results and got along well with her bosses. She had a big mouth, though (still does, truth be told), and since it was a tough corporate culture, Kim often shared her complaints about management's practices with her peers. From her perspective, it was obviously a tough environment, and they all needed to blow off a little steam now and then, which they often did after work. She assumed her coworkers felt the same way—that is, until the day she got called in to the general manager's office, where he showed her a list of things she had said and when she had said them and wanted to know what her problem was.

She was stunned. Someone had been collecting evidence against her and reporting on her to her superiors. Who disliked her this much? Who had stabbed her in the back? She never found out, but it didn't matter because she learned the bigger lesson. Keep your mouth shut. Complaining isn't good for an organization and big mouths don't get ahead.

avoiding and resolving conflict

The effects of conflict in the workplace are widespread and costly. Studies have shown that anywhere between 24 and 60 percent of management time and energy is spent dealing with anger. Anger leads to decreased productivity, increased stress, hampered performance, high turnover rate, absenteeism, and, at its most extreme, violence and death. Conflict in the workplace can result from a number of factors and can be individual- or group-focused. Competition between departments is as common as disputes between individuals. The easiest way to resolve conflict is to avoid it in first place. Here's how to do it:

1. **Communicate:** Conflict happens when people aren't on the same page. Strong leaders communicate the goals of the organization and work with individuals. They have an acknowledged system for accountability and everyone is treated the same way.

2. **Listen:** Make sure you hear what the people are saying—acknowledge their challenges and make sure you provide the support and resources they need to accomplish their goals.

3. **Set boundaries:** You can be professional, empathetic, and compassionate toward your employees without crossing the line of becoming their friend.

4. **Nip it in the bud.** If you notice tempers or voices rising, address the situation as soon as possible. Listening isn't enough; you must offer a solution so that the conflict doesn't repeat itself.

the power of positive gossip

Malicious gossip is such a powerful and pervasive problem in our society that there is actually a national effort to reduce it called Words Can Heal (www.wordscanheal.org). Their mission is to promote the value and practice of ethical speech in order to improve our democracy and build mutual respect, honor, and dignity in our country. They have created a pledge that's worth repeating:

- I pledge to think more about the words I use.
- I will try to see how gossip hurts people, including myself, and work to eliminate it from my life.
- I will try to replace words that hurt with words that encourage, engage, and enrich.
- I will not become discouraged when I am unable to choose words perfectly, because making the world a better place is hard work.
- And I am pledging to do that, one word at a time.

Their pledge underscores how powerful words are and the importance of choosing positive ones. It's very easy to gossip—especially in the workplace. Words Can Heal even created a training package for the workplace and their number one recommendation for stopping workplace gossip is "Bite your tongue before you gossip; your tongue may hurt, but your colleagues and reputation won't."

We're not sure we've ever gone an entire day at our various jobs without a good old gossip session. It's one of our favorite ways to blow off steam. But after reading the research and seeing what an uphill battle women already face, we're going to sign the pledge and turn gossip into a good thing. What if women in the workplace chose to pass along only positive gossip or none at all? Would we further our cause? Would we change the general perception of our leadership skills? We're guessing we would, and for our part, we're going to try.

whatever you do . . . don't write it down

It can never be said enough, e-mail and instant messaging can be dangerous tools. Organizations monitor e-mails and they can be saved forever. Before you hit send, you had better be sure you've double-checked both what you've written and to whom you are sending. It only takes one erroneous "reply all" to learn that message the hard way.

We were at a production company having a meeting and noticed a big commotion in the office. When we asked what was up, we were told that one of their competitors had sent a mass e-mail of good news to a number of broadcasters and other production companies. The e-mail was itself benign and usually something you'd scan and delete. Apparently the sender hadn't thought to blind-copy everyone because, a moment later, a well-known executive at a major broadcaster "replied to all" that he wanted to be removed from the mailing list . . . he was getting too much junk mail. And then a crazy thing happened. One by one, people on the mailing list began replying that they too wanted to be taken off; pretty soon fifty messages had popped up in people's in-boxes with requests to be deleted from this rival company's newsletter. The company was humiliated in front of their clients and their customers.

Girls, take heed: Instant Messaging can be even more danger-ous, because it's very easy to be chatting in one window at one mo-ment and in another the next. The nature of the communication is quick and short, and if you're writing something you don't want oth-ers to see, you had better be darn sure you know who's computer screen it's popping up on. Also, a number of companies are making it against company policy to IM—so check into the rules before you load up the software.

modern office etiquette

We were fortunate to learn our manners from our mothers, but many weren't so lucky. When we decided to include a "Modern Of-fice Etiquette," section we went to the source. Kim's mother, Sharyn Yorio, not only taught her well, but in her consulting practice, Sus-tainable Marketing, Inc., she spends many days teaching architects and engineers social graces and good old-fashioned manners. She shared her top tips with us.

- Use business language in all communication, even e-mails. I don't want to see slang, even if you have a familiar relationship with someone. Some cringe-worthy examples include "like" and "yeah."
- A personal hand-written note is worth its weight in gold. Write it immediately after meeting someone so they can receive it the next day. It doesn't have to be lengthy, but it does need to be in your own hand. People get so many e-mails that the thank-you one just gets buried.

- Say "please" and "thank you." I can't believe I have to remind people of that one.
- Investigate how your employer would like you to answer your phone. I've found every place has its own standard. I answer with my name.
- If you're using your cell phone for work and you don't recognize the number, use your professional greeting.
- If your employer has a company manual, make sure you've read it. There will be important information as to how they want you to conduct yourself in their place of business.

SOME TIPS FOR OPEN OFFICES

Many offices are open plan, and while they are supposed to foster collaborative processes, without a little common courtesy on everyone's part they will foster plain old bad feelings.

- When on the phone or having a chat with a colleague, try to keep your voice in a conversational tone. Loud talkers are distracting to the people around them.
- Keep your work area neat and orderly. Be prepared for unexpected visitors. You never want to embarrass your employer or your colleagues with your sloppiness.
- If you overhear a conversation between other people, don't butt in and offer your two cents. For the most part, if they wanted your opinion they would ask. If you feel it's imperative to offer your opinion, then make a note to yourself and mention something after the meeting or send along an e-mail with your thoughts. Your colleagues will appreciate you respecting their space.
- Don't use the speakerphone. Headsets are a good option because you can talk softly directly into them. Just don't buy the cheap ones, because you'll end up shouting to be heard.

- Respect people's space. Don't use someone's phone or borrow something off a desk without asking. Just because it's out in the open doesn't mean it is open for the taking.
- If there are common areas such as conference rooms, make sure you sign up in advance and respect the schedule.
- If there are common areas such as kitchens, clean up after yourself.
- Don't answer your cell phone during the office hours unless you know it's a business call. Keep your ringer low or off, so you don't disturb others.

the dress code that goes everywhere

Outfit anxiety ranks right up there with the fear of public speaking. Many might not consider it a "fear" in line with the rest of those discussed in our fears chapter, but it can be a big cause of stress and even a little panic each morning. How many times have you been late to work because you hated every outfit you tried on that morning? Nothing feels right, fits right, or makes the right statement. You're left sweating in your underwear staring at the piles of clothes that just don't work. You pull on the least hideous option and hope for the best.

What's a girl to do when she always wants to look her best? How can you be outfitted perfectly for the job every day without a stylist, super-model physique, and zillion-dollar wardrobe budget? It's not as difficult as you think. With a simple rule and our "Dress Code that Goes Everywhere," your outfit anxiety will be a thing of the past.

The first rule should be the most obvious: dress for the job you want, not the job you have. Men do this very well and it's easier for them. When a man pulls on a suit he achieves instant credibility and respect. Women don't have that kind of luck. Suits for women are a tricky situation. It is difficult to find the right suit or one that fits properly. And just wearing a suit doesn't instantly translate as it does for men. We have to figure things out and be a little creative. We have to pay attention. One way is to note what the best-dressed and most-respected women above you are wearing and model yourself after them (even if you have to do it on a smaller budget). You will project the same credibility as the women at the job level you seek.

"DRESS CODE THAT GOES EVERYWHERE"

- When in doubt, go black. A black pants suit, a black dress, a black skirt with any kind of top works everywhere for every occasion. Throw in some black shoes, and without even thinking, you're perfect.
- Natural fibers always. Stay away from rayon, acetate, or anything shiny—they look terrible and make you sweat. With wool and cotton you can never go wrong.
- Grooming goes a long way. Get a regular manicure or do it yourself. Nude lasts longer and chips don't show. Save the dark colors for your toes. Keep your eyebrows waxed, threaded, or plucked. Keep hair split-end free, and when overdue for a haircut or color, just pull it back into a ponytail.
- Shoes make the woman and there's a pair to fit any size—something you cannot say about expensive designer jeans. Keep your shoes in good condition. Get soles and heels repaired and keep them shined. Especially boots.
- Go ahead, strap on the highest heels you can attractively walk in. People should notice the shoe, not the trouble you're having walking across the office.
- One suit is probably enough—but make sure it's tailored. We've never met anyone who can fit a suit "off the rack."
- No bare midriffs, ever. We love tank tops and hate tummies.

- Keep the tattoos under cover. Keep the undergarments under cover. And for God's sake make sure you wear undergarments—no one needs a Britney Spears moment.
- Wear day clothes during the day and evening clothes at night. We worked with a woman who wore taffeta skirts with matching shoes and halter tops to work and we could never figure out if she hadn't gone home from the night before.
- Check out the magazines. We love *InStyle*'s fashion coverage. They give you a number of options for all shapes, sizes, and budgets.
- Wear makeup—you'll look better. It doesn't have to be heavy. Just a little foundation, blush, and mascara will do the trick.

girl taking charge

SARAH BURKE, THE VICE PRESIDENT OF SALES AND MARKETING AT THE DEVELOPERS GROUP

Sarah Burke always wanted a fulfilling career and initially pursued acting. She thought she was a good actress, but the roles just weren't coming, so when she couldn't ignore her lack of success anymore, she sat down and reevaluated her priorities and goals. She didn't make a step-by-step plan, but she knew the direction she wanted in her new chosen profession—real estate.

At first, real estate was just the day job that financed her acting passion, but she soon discovered that she had a real knack for it. She also had good timing. She started during the rental boom in '99. The company she was working for got their first on-site rental building and asked her to be one of the agents. She took the position knowing that it would open many doors in a niche of the industry that was difficult to break into. When the project was over the company didn't want to lose her, and within six months she was made the director of one of their offices—at twenty-five!

Her experience and ability to learn quickly made her extremely marketable in a cutthroat industry. She decided to try her luck on the open market, started interviewing, received several offers, and took a position as a project manager for a brand-new company.

As a project manager Sarah oversaw a team of people—all older than she. And the combination of her actual age and her young looks made it extremely difficult to be taken seriously and turned her workplace into a political minefield. She managed a staff of forty people who wouldn't fill her in on what they were doing because they didn't think they had to—even though it was her responsibility to know what they were doing. And she also had to navigate her managers. It was a small new company and there was a crisis every day. She has learned a lot about getting through politically charged situations over the past ten years and here is her advice:

- Don't yell at anyone because it doesn't get you anywhere. Even if you are right.
- Don't talk yourself up; prove yourself through action.
- If you want to win loyalty with a skeptical staff, solve a few problems for them.
- Be a friendly bitch. Really, I know it sounds funny, but what I mean is that be tough for your people when they need you to be. Stick up for them, and be willing to be the bad guy.
- Pick your battles. If someone really wants to do it their way, voice your point of view but let them. Even if you know it is wrong. Because when they come to you afterward to fix it, you will have earned their respect.
- And when it comes to sharing your age, never lie and never tell!

a view from the ladder

Linda Malkin has worked in the health care industry for more than thirty years, first as a nurse, then in the malpractice department of a New York City–based insurance company and for a major New York hospital in what we know today as risk management. She is currently the director of risk management and claims services at the Valley Hospital in Ridgewood, New Jersey—a top job in her field.

We know Linda as a generous and nurturing force in our life, as well as the mother of Amie and Laurie, two of our favorite Girl's Guide contributors. Linda is a gracious host and a loving wife. It turns out she's also one tough cookie at work, where she learned long ago that if you can't find the power in the organization, you're not going to get very far. She came up through the ranks during a time when very few women were in senior positions and the women who had fought their way up the ladder were not giving up their positions to anyone—especially not another woman.

Her lessons in office politics might sound a bit harsh, but Linda is not only someone we trust with our careers, but has enough experience that you dismiss this advice at your own risk. Take heed, girls, this is how the big boys play.

Lessons from Linda, a.k.a. Everything you needed to know about office politics but nobody would tell you

- **Find the power.** It's never enough to do good work for your direct boss alone. You can't be sure that person will actually give you the credit you deserve. To get ahead you must make sure the real people in power know you and what you're doing. So the first step is to figure out who holds the power. Is it your boss or your boss's boss? Two levels up? Perhaps a department over from you? Assessing which manager or department has the power to get you a raise or promoted is a key step toward achieving your goal. The sad fact is if you play by the rules, you'll never get ahead. It's your income and your future; don't let anybody mess with them.

- **Build bridges to upper management.** Once you know who's in charge, explore ways to introduce your skills and talents to them. In the early '90s, I worked in the malpractice division of a large inner-city teaching hospital. All of the managers were women who had to fight their way into these jobs—and they were not about to help a sister out. My direct supervisor was one of the worst offenders. Pretty quickly I realized how to get ahead in this organization: I was going to have to do an end-run around her. So I did, but it's important to mention that I was doing exemplary work. I wasn't using politics to get ahead without deserving it; I was just making sure that I got credit for the work I generated. My supervisor took credit for all of my work as a matter of course and I figured out how to make it stop. I had the opportunity to drive my boss's boss home every night. She was on my way, and during our little chats I was able to champion my accomplishments. I never gossiped or spoke ill of my manager; we simply talked about work and she figured out that I was working at a higher level than I was being given credit for and she compensated me for it.
- **Make yourself indispensable and make sure that more than your boss knows it.** Work hard to figure out the culture you're in and what kind of contribution will make you shine, and then do everything you can within the confines of ethical boundaries to do it. Try to provide a work product that they never knew they needed—until you showed it to them. I had one position where I became the de facto spokesperson for the company. Senior management would call on me to be the public face of the organization. I gave presentations, went to receptions, and entertained important clients. My boss's bosses knew I was someone who could be counted on *not* to embarrass, and I became invaluable.
- **Break the pattern and plan for the future.** I have painted a pretty tough picture, but it doesn't have to continue. I have

seen women become more secure over the past thirty years, having earned their power, so they can now be more generous and collaborative. My current direct and senior bosses, both women, use their intellect, wit, and style to support and nurture (which would have been unheard of thirty years ago). I also think that high-achieving women now also have husbands (or not) and children, making them more sensitive to juggling child care issues and family emergencies. I teach everyone around me everything I know. We prioritize succession planning. It's a cultural expectation of my employer that I will have someone in place who can replace me and I am expected to (and enjoy) training them to do the job as well, if not better, than I have when I am gone.

nine

big thinking

Plodding along without looking around you and above you will keep you stuck in junior-level positions or worse in a job that doesn't thrill you. Be proactive. Investigate how your assignment fits into the bigger picture of the project. Figure out how your role fits into the efficiency of the team. How is your company doing in relation to its competitors? Is your industry booming or has the bubble burst? Remember, you are just a piece of a bigger puzzle.

When you start expanding your view of your job/career/industry, you will be in a position to begin making "promotion-worthy" suggestions. In this chapter we will challenge you to start thinking bigger about yourself and your career by learning how to manage your boss, making the most of working weekends, making a big impression at the next company event, and building a bigger profile within your organization.

influencing upward

If you asked the team members of a health care executive we know, each of them would say that this executive had single-handedly saved the company. She kept the staff from quitting because of over-work and developed new business in a time of transition. If you interviewed her clients, they would tell you the same thing. And yet her management did not identify her as a top leader, and asked her to step down. Why? She was so busy solving problems that she forgot to put her head up and into the boss's office to share her achievements.

Bad relationships with your boss or poor communication will hurt your career. This is true for the most junior employees and even some of the best managers, the ones who continually motivate their staff but forget that their own careers need nurturing too. Your relationship with your boss is a key to success for you and your team. It's not exclusively about ego-stroking (although some of it is). If your boss doesn't know what you're doing, (or doesn't like what you're doing), then you might as well not be doing it at all.

"Managing up" means focusing on the relationship with your boss to obtain the best results for you, your boss, and your organization. It also means getting what you need from your boss in order to do your job well. Actively managing your relationship maximizes both your ability and your boss's ability to contribute to the organization, and it helps you weather the inevitable conflicts that will occur. Your supervisor has critical information and an organizational perspective that you need in order to perform your job while staying in line with your company's growth and direction. She can (and should) share developments that occur at higher levels in your company and can update you on priorities. Your boss can connect you with other areas in the organization, and can serve as your advocate when you need resources and cooperation from other departments or divisions.

Understanding your boss's goals, priorities, and work style are key factors in your success. Value your boss's time and be strategic when you're asking for it—don't bring the boss problems. Bring solutions and recommendations. If you've solved a big problem, don't downplay your role.

Whenever possible, flex your style to accommodate your boss. We had a junior member on staff who drove us crazy because she injected no enthusiasm into her delivery of information. We spoke to her about it several times and asked her to work on her communication skills. She seemed otherwise competent and worked extremely hard, but she had a voice that telegraphed (to us at least) that she wasn't engaged. We were hard on her out of frustration and distrust. We could have completely misread the situation and in fact she may have been fully engaged in what she was doing, but she did herself a disservice by not communicating in a way that made us comfortable.

working weekends works for you

The fact is many of us will spend at least a few weekends at the office catching up. In many cases it's the only way to keep up. When we were just starting out in public relations, Saturdays at the agency were a given and the same group of go-getter, bleary-eyed, junior-level colleagues showed up after a late Friday night with an egg sandwich and coffee in hand each week.

If you like what you do and feel appreciated for the extra effort, then putting in weekend time at the office isn't the end of the world. (A caveat: don't procrastinate during the week because you know that you will be coming in during your personal time.) Saturdays at the office need to be highly productive. Enjoy them if you can and make sure you let management know you were there without looking like a kiss ass.

Start with a realistic list of tasks to accomplish. When making the list, include all of the projects that would benefit from quiet time. We come in to write. New business proposals, blogs, press releases all benefit from peace and quiet. We also come in to think—something we forget to do when the phones are ringing and e-mails are filling our in-boxes. Weekends at the office are blessedly quiet and a great time to focus without constant interruption.

Even though you are at the office, the weekend is actually your time, so try to make it as enjoyable as possible. Bring in music and snacks. We have a few guilty pleasures music-wise, and when we are typing away in the deserted office we always pull out the Beastie Boys.

Getting credit for your weekend time is tricky. You want your boss to know that you are putting in the extra time, but you don't want to appear to be a brownnoser. Unfortunately, if you are in a senior position, then the overtime might be expected, so call attention to it only if it is highly unusual for you to come in or if you completed a high-profile assignment over the weekend. You also don't want the rest of the staff to be aware that you are tooting your own horn. They will resent you for it, especially if they were working right next to you.

A few methods of letting your boss know that you were at your desk when everyone else was at the beach:

- Send an e-mail from your desktop. It will be date/time stamped and not come from your BlackBerry.
- Leave a new document (proposal, article, business plan) on her desk for her to find first thing Monday morning.
- During your next one-on-one meeting, mention something that you read, discovered, or thought of over the weekend. Even if they don't know that you were in the office, they will get the idea that work is on your mind.

bring it on: more responsibility, please

Most people who get promoted are already doing the job above them on the ladder, so to get that promotion you have your eye on, take on more. Taking on additional responsibilities is an opportunity to learn your job more quickly; you can also offer to take on tasks that bring in other departments and vendors to widen your network. However you work it out, by offering to do more you will be making a great impression on your boss.

Sandy Lish, principal/founder of The Castle Group, Inc., says that "We should volunteer for more responsibility if we want to move ahead. By volunteering, rather than waiting to be asked, we show that we're ready for new challenges, that we have the confidence and abilities necessary to move ahead, and that we are fully engaged in our own careers. Proactivity, not passivity, reaps rewards." It is easy to get so caught up in your own work that you assume that your supervisor somehow knows that you are ready for additional challenges. That's just simply not the case. Your boss has her own set of concerns, projects, and meetings to prepare for. She also has her own career to take care of, so you need to speak up for yourself and tell her that you are ready and excited about taking on more.

building up your professional profile

After speaking to a wide range of women about their thoughts on what it takes to succeed, we found the general consensus to be that if you want to shine at a company, you have to build a high profile. Having a high profile means that most people at an organization know who you are and what you bring to the table. We encourage you to spend time on professional profile-building because it means that you are working toward setting yourself apart from your peers in the eyes of the decision makers. After you have proven your value to your company, asking for that raise, promotion, bigger office, better assignments, additional staff, and anything else, becomes infinitely easier. Sure, it seems like doing a good job should be enough, but the truth is that women have to spend more time than men on this type of interoffice public relations.

Here's how to raise your profile:

- Become an expert on something in your field.
- Create a blog (just don't bash the company or share work-related secrets).
- Always challenge yourself.
- Take on high-profile and high-risk projects whenever possible.
- Market your successes to your boss.
- Do more than is asked and sometimes more than is needed.
- Volunteer to represent the company at a public event, workshop, or conference.
- Write articles in trade publications.
- Offer to coordinate a brown bag lunch series with guest speakers.
- Start a mentoring program for the company.

conferences, retreats, black-tie, oh my

Work is social. Holiday parties, corporate retreats, occasional black-tie events, client dinners, and retirement parties all require us to put our best foot forward. These social offshoots of office life offer opportunities to shine—or fall flat on our faces. Because social situations are less controlled than the workplace, they are complicated to navigate. More attention is paid to your likeability, which makes it tough for the shy among us to shine. Think about who shines at the holiday party—it is often the person with the biggest personality and not the one with the biggest results. Since there are different rules for the time outside of the office, these suggestions will help you excel even in the most awkward situations.

CONFERENCES

When sent to a conference for your company, there are two times to make a great impression: at the conference itself and when you get back to the office. To set yourself up for success on-site, do your research. Know who is going with you from your team, review the schedule so you know what to expect, make appointments in advance to meet with key attendees, and bring a list of recommended restaurants. Being the one with the answers will help even the most socially uncomfortable feel a little more confident. When you get back from the conference, send a report to your boss about what you learned and contributed, and what you would like to share with the group. You were sent to the conference on company money; prove that you were worth the investment.

CORPORATE RETREATS

We had a boss who invited the entire company out to her house for a retreat every summer. The house was near the beach and every year came the requisite volleyball game. You can only imagine the tension. We had to play in our bathing suits, against our managers, with the owner of the company, who was an admirably competitive spirit. Make no mistake, we were not the best players on the team, but our positive attitude was a bonus. The key to building your profile up during corporate retreats is to make an effort to have fun, be a joiner (not always easy for some of us), have a good attitude, and always be aware that your behavior off-site will be remembered on-site. So that means limit the drinking, swearing, and overall silliness.

BLACK-TIE EVENTS

Once a year we go to the industry black-tie event. When we encourage our staff to make the most of this event, we are really telling them to justify the $275 spent on their ticket. Sad, but true. If your company has invited you to a high-profile, ticketed event, you better make the most of the opportunity. It begins with your outfit. We suggest something stunning, classic, and not too sexy. High heels, simple jewelry, and nice hair and makeup round it out. The pressure is on to be a good dinner companion, so brush up on your current events and be ready to talk about a wide range of topics. Find out the seating chart before hand, and if you are lucky enough to be seated next to a senior member of the team, then share some business ideas.

Be yourself, just a more professional version. Talk, share ideas, listen, and be on your very best social behavior. And never forget that you are being judged (maybe more so) when you're off the clock.

the importance of chiming in

If you are the one at the staff meeting who doesn't say anything, know this—people will start to wonder why you are there. Those who don't say a word are more conspicuous after a while than the bigmouths. And the longer you wait to jump in, the more you will be scrutinized by the group when you finally do. Take it from us and all of the bosses we interviewed for our second book: everyone is included in a meeting for a reason, and it isn't just to look pretty (although we always do). You are there because you are an important member of the team and what you have to say is relevant.

Wendy Bengal, an account director for Sanders\Wingo Advertising's El Paso office and vice chair of the Texas Commission for Women, learned the hard way that it is essential to speak up.

When my husband's career relocated us to a smaller market, I left a fifteen-year career in public relations and found a job in advertising. As with any big change, it took a while to build confidence in an unfamiliar area. I let my unfamiliarity with industry details eclipse the communication skills and instincts I built in another area. For several weeks I held my tongue in meetings when my gut feeling urged me to speak, only to hear the same comment coming out of someone else's mouth later. I missed chance after chance to prove my worth. Finally, I realized that I didn't have to act like the new kid just because I was in that slot. I spoke up; realizing if it went against some unknown industry code, they would fill me in. In the end, it was that outside point of view they were looking for, and taking those chances to speak my mind is what established my position in the agency.

Because you don't want to say something just for the sake of saying it, learn enough about your company and industry to have a useful thought, idea, or opinion to contribute. Do your homework and draft questions you could ask or statements you could make. It will be scary at first, so ease into it by making it a goal to say one thing at the next meeting and then maybe ask a question in the meeting after that. An easy way to get your feet wet is by backing up the contributions of others with a word of support; a "good idea" or "we should try that" sprinkled in never hurts. It sounds corny, but it will be appreciated by your coworker and good deeds are often reciprocated. There's a good chance they will back you when you finally throw your big idea into the ring.

promotions: the warning on the label

We're all coached to believe that promotions are the golden ring on the carousel. And why not? Isn't it always better to have a more impressive title? Doesn't more money automatically accompany a more senior-level position? Contrary to popular belief, sometimes it is better to pass on a promotion. Whenever you are offered a promotion, find out as many details as possible before accepting or declining even though your instinct at the time will most likely be to scream *yes!*

When offered a promotion, why in the world would you ever say no? Because you absolutely need to know what is going to be expected of you if you take this job. After six months at a special events company, Allison Rainy had befriended her manager and asked him what his job entailed. He told her that in addition to running events, he was expected to bring in new clients to add to his portfolio and maintain a certain amount in billings. "I just didn't like what I was doing enough to hustle like that, but I was glad that I found out what my future would look like there. I could have wasted years working toward something I didn't enjoy." Read the fine print of any job promotion.

Many senior-level positions have additional travel involved, so you want to do some digging. Will you be required to attend conferences to represent your company? Are you going to be expected to relocate to oversee new business? Will you need to go to out-of-state clients on a regular basis? If you are without a lot of personal responsibilities, then additional business travel is a great learning experience and can be a great deal of fun, but if you have children it can be a strain, so make sure you have enough help at home before you go on the road.

You also want to find out if the promotion comes with a raise.

Most of us assume that of course you would get a raise if you are doing more work, but that isn't always the case. We know of two people in our circle who were given very impressive titles without the money attached. One was promised a raise in six months, the other wasn't given one at all. Before you accept the position, you may want to find out what others at that level are making in your industry and try to negotiate a little. You don't want to be four months into the new job and already resenting it because you feel used.

When discussing the title with your boss, try to find out what the goals are for the team and what you will be responsible for. That information will help you decide if you have access to the right people to get the job done. If you are going to have sales goals, then you want to make sure you have a crackerjack sales force under your umbrella. If you realize that the team you will soon be leading needs major revamping, then make sure you discuss your right to hire and fire.

When considering a new job, you will also need to assess your professional skill set because the promotion may require you to learn new ones. Oftentimes, public speaking becomes an important aspect of an executive's career or the ability to read a profit-and-loss statement. Whatever the specific tools of your trade may be, know what you need to know.

Consider if this promotion will make you vulnerable to a layoff. Are you aware of how your company is doing in general? Is it profitable? Are shareholders happy (if public)? Are the owners happy (if private)? Are there many people at the company with your title and similar responsibilities? If so, you may be considered redundant. Does your group have a healthy budget or is it being slashed? Are the higher-ups focused on what your group generates? And the crucial question: does your area of expertise generate money for your company or spend it?

Be clear about how you will be spending your day before you take a promotion. We had a friend who was offered a huge promotion, quickly becoming a vice president shortly after being hired as a director at a very large mental health group. Little did she know (because she was blinded by the title) that she was being hired to be the hatchet woman for the organization. Most of her job for the first six months was firing people, day after day after day. We ran into her soon after her one-year anniversary and we asked how things were going. She told us, "You know, sometimes more money and a better title just isn't worth it."

girl taking charge

Deborah Blackwell, executive vice president and general manager of SOAPnet, is committed to helping others succeed, in part because she was mentored by some of the strongest and most successful women in television. Fresh out of Harvard Business School, Deborah landed a job on the financial side of the entertainment business, but it wasn't her true calling. She had an undergraduate degree in English and wanted to spend her days doing something creative, not just running numbers. Breaking into the creative side of the business after ten years on the business end wasn't easy, but she was determined and left New York City for Los Angeles. When she arrived in Hollywood, she had the smarts, natural skill, and ambition, but she was "as green as they come." Judy Palone, then president of Hearst Entertainment, gave her a job and taught her everything she knew about the business. Once she became a development executive she informally created a network of women in her industry who helped one another by sharing professional information, advice, contacts, and support. When we asked her what she would share with women about taking charge of their careers, she told us this story:

I have always considered myself to be a fair boss and will go the extra mile for my employees whenever possible, so I was surprised one day when my assistant told me the reason she was quitting was—me. And if that didn't throw me enough, she then told me that she was quitting the entertainment business to go into the foreign service. When I pressed her for details on her thinking she said, "Deborah, you love your job so much and you are so passionate about what you do I realized that I just don't feel the same way. I need to find something that I feel that way about. When I started thinking about where I started and remembered how happy I was in college earning my political science degree, I knew that's the direction I had to go in."

So here is what I want everyone to take away from this story: find a job in an industry that you are passionate about. That should be your starting point. If you love your job you will be energized by it, you will be inspired by it, and in turn will energize and inspire those around you. I only started setting the world on fire when I found my passion. I was making a very good salary on the financial side of things, and took a huge pay cut when I changed over to creative, but because I loved what I did and was good at it, it took me only two years to outearn myself. So don't be afraid to think big and take risks when finding your passion.

a view from the ladder

Lori is one of our favorite corporate girls. She loves the big company and has been on the fast track her entire career. She devoted ten years to her last employer, rising from a junior staff member to a managing director. During that time, she lived in three different cities and two different countries.

Then came a time when change in management had her questioning her future with the organization and, worse, her abilities. After six months of soul-searching and six months of job-hunting, she has now landed her dream job. Lori shares with us a few lessons she learned in one of the most challenging, yet ultimately successful, years of her career.

How do you know when you're ready for the next big career challenge?

Life's too short not to love what you do. If you find yourself complaining about your work life on a regular basis and you have not been able to address your issues with your current employers, then it may be time to move on. The caveat is that sometimes it is best to stick it out in a particular role if you think additional time will place you in a better position when it comes time to move— for example, by completing a big assignment that you'll be able to highlight in job interviews.

Can you share some successful strategies for managing up?

Strategy #1: Managing up is like managing any customer or client. Respect their time and need for efficiency. Respect their need to have a say in what you're doing by being a good listener and being responsive to their views.

Strategy #2: Candor and collegiality go hand in hand. Life is easy when your bosses agree with everything you're doing, but more challenging when they don't. You need to find a style that enables you to advance your point, own up to mistakes, or "agree to disagree" while minimizing tension—even when your bosses lose their cool themselves.

Strategy #3: Protect your bosses from surprises. Most would rather know where things stand and what your solutions are than be caught off guard with bad news.

When your confidence is rocked, what steps can you take to regain it?

Every career girl should build a network of confidants and mentors that they consult. If you have a strong mentor outside of your own organization, he or she can give you much-needed, objective perspective on how/when to address a negative job situation, how/when to remove yourself from a negative job situation, your strengths, and your growth areas.

asking for what you deserve

Here is another work world secret . . . everyone is counting on you *not* asking for what you deserve. If you don't ask for a raise, the company saves money. If you don't ask for a promotion, then the organization doesn't have to reconfigure the staff. If you don't ask for an office, then the company doesn't have to find one for you. The ones who ask (and not enough of them are women) are the folks who end up fairly compensated and fully staffed. This chapter will help you face the challenge of negotiating for a work situation that works for you, beginning with helping you identify what you need followed by the steps for asking for it.

be the squeaky wheel

Your boss, client, or coworker doesn't have ESP, so if you don't ask for that vacant office, higher retainer, or day off, you won't get it. As an employee, especially a busy one, it is hard to remember that the company you work for doesn't usually volunteer raises, promotions, better working situations, flextime, days off, or job shares. Any change to your position that will benefit mostly you needs to be initiated by you.

While researching this book we read an article by a male boss who said he noticed that he thought of men first when considering promotions and raises because they were often the ones who had been the loudest and had badgered him the most about making more money. He also wrote that many of the women who came and spoke to him about their careers focused the discussion on what they could do for the company rather than what the company could do for them. While he wrote that he respected the work ethic of the women he employed, he still most often rewarded his male employees. Sound familiar? As women, most of us are concerned with the well-being of the team. We don't want to put people in an uncomfortable position by asking for something; we don't want to appear to be bragging and we are more concerned with how we can do a better job.

We are too focused on the smaller picture, the day-to-day of doing our jobs, and other times we are just too afraid to ask. But whatever the reasons for us not piping up, we are losing out on the money, power, and positions and the bigmouths are reaping the rewards.

Do everything you can to get a "yes" by thinking through exactly what you are asking for and why you deserve it ahead of time. But most important, be ready to explain in detail (sometimes with numbers to back you up) why what you are asking for benefits the company. Be prepared to answer what it will do for the organization if you get what you want. Because at the end of the day, even if you are the best employee they have ever had, it's all about what is best for the business.

the "everyone wins" negotiation

Whether you notice or not, you negotiate almost every single day. Weaving in and out of traffic is a negotiation with other drivers, navigating busy supermarkets, passing chores back and forth with your partner, all unremarkable yet familiar negotiations that hopefully don't get confrontational. However, when it comes to a negotiation at work, all of a sudden asking for what you want from someone else is fraught with anxiety. The secret to a successful negotiation is for both parties to walk away with something. A positive outcome is always a win-win. If there is residual resentment on either side, then it wasn't successful. If you're asking for a raise, you want more money, but the company or client wants to get more for that money, so you need to show them how that will be the case.

DO NOT BE CONFRONTATIONAL
This aggressive stance will cause your boss to be defensive, and that is not helpful for a productive exchange. Approach the negotiation as a conversation. Simply lay out what you need and want in order to do a better job.

KEEP EMOTION OUT OF IT
If you go into a negotiation angry, you will get that back. If you go into it teary, then you are undermining your credibility. The best approach is a non-emotional one where it's just the facts. Practicing first helps.

PUT YOURSELF IN THEIR SHOES
To help plan for the negotiation, take the time to mentally put yourself in their position. And try to look at your request objectively. It should help you determine if you are asking for something insane or insanely reasonable.

IT'S NOT PERSONAL
No matter what the results are of the negotiation, it isn't personal. Sure, if they like you, then the conversation will be easier, but you will get what you are asking for only if it makes sense for the company.

ASK FOR THEIR POINT OF VIEW
It is helpful, even if the answer is "no," to get a better understanding from your boss about her questions and concerns. So, even before you get the final answer, ask what her initial thoughts are about your request.

OFFER SOLUTIONS
Be proactive about addressing any concerns you think your boss may have.

SHOW UP WITH THE BOTTOM LINE
Good business dictates to give you what you are asking for if it benefits the company, so come to the meeting armed with hard numbers that support your case.

IT'S ABOUT THEM
When you are asking for something, don't forget to keep the conversation focused on the company. For instance, if you are asking for a promotion, focus on how you would use the clout that accompanies the new title to bring in additional clients.

THERE IS A RIGHT TIME AND A WRONG TIME

Make sure you are having the negotiation at a good time. And we are talking about a good time in the very broadest sense—a good time of day, your reputation at a good point, your boss in a good mood, the company making some good money. A truly good time.

DON'T FORCE IT DOWN THEIR THROATS

If they are just not getting what you are asking for or don't want to give it to you at that time, don't force it. Pushing it will only throw your chances of going back and asking again out the window.

GIVE A LITTLE

Come in ready to make a few concessions and know what you are willing to give up. Holding on to only one outcome to make you happy is not a negotiation.

the benefits of asking

The most obvious benefit to asking for something is that you may actually get what you want. And you will learn a little about your place in the company during the process. But the biggest benefit to asking for something on your own behalf is that it forces you to grow.

could i have more money?

The bottom line is this: the company doesn't want to give you more money. They want you to do the job you are doing for the same amount, if not less. Some organizations issue cost-of-living raises annually, which is basically them getting away with giving you the least amount possible. And some companies will give raises only when you are holding them over a barrel by threatening to leave. The point is that asking your boss for money is a tricky conversation to have. To help you plan, we have outlined some key tips to get you started on your "raise proposal."

Lay the groundwork for a raise. If you wait until your annual review, then your boss is already expecting the request, so she is ready with a number that she will proactively offer. Additionally, if you wait until the review, then you are going to have very little wiggle room because the budget at that point is pretty set. We recommend you start working toward a raise three to six months in advance.

Start keeping track of your major contributions and successes on a running list. If you landed a big client, reached a sales goal, hired a superstar employee, or saved the company money, then add it to the list. Remember to e-mail your boss updates of any major successes so that she is aware of what you are contributing.

Since this request is a financial one, figure out what money you bring in or save the company. This is easy if you are in sales but less straightforward for most of us. When Caitlin was in publishing she asked for a raise based on the success of a few key books she had worked on. She didn't get the books into the bookstore for the company, but as a publicist she got the authors on the *Today* show, which in turn helped sell the books off the shelves of that bookstore. Beyond the publicity successes, she could point to how well her assistant was trained and beginning to generate some great work. Remember, if your job is to manage a team, then include their contribution, too.

Consider a formal document. Megan Walker went to her boss with a fully fleshed-out proposal of where she saw her career going, contributions she had made, how she impacted the bottom line of the company, and the additional responsibilities she would like to take on. "It worked. They gave me 10 percent over the 15 percent raise I had asked for."

Timing is everything. Many people believe that waiting until the annual review is the right time, but asking when there is "good buzz" on you, the company is making a profit, and you are in good stead with the team is critical to your success.

How much to ask for is pretty unique to your situation, but be reasonable, and whatever you do, don't ask for a cost-of-living raise. No one wants to hear that you need to make more money because you just bought a bigger house. You will get a raise because you deserve to make more money for the hard work that you do or you will get a raise because everyone doing your job elsewhere makes more. A good place to start is www.salary.com, where you can get a rough idea of what people in your position are making. It might be worth attending a few networking events so you can discreetly ask around to see what the average salaries are. Reading trade publications or speaking to headhunters are other ways to find out what people are making.

When should you not ask? When the market is crashing, the customers are disgruntled, you just made a big mistake, you have been at the company for only six months, your boss is just about to be fired, or you are planning on quitting even if they give you a raise.

could i have a better title?

Emily Hart wanted a promotion. She had been at her job for a year and felt that she deserved it. At her annual review she raised the issue but was shut down, because when she was asked by her boss why she should have the promotion, her answer was "Because I have been here a year." Being anywhere for a year, two years, or ten years is not a reason to be promoted. Doing a great job, taking on responsibilities that go beyond your required scope, and proving loyalty to the company are reasons for promotion. Sandy Lish, founder of The Castle Group, Inc., told us, "The best time to ask for a promotion is when you're already proving you can do the job above you. At my company, we tend to promote people who are already working, in some ways, at the next level. Just being proficient at your job doesn't mean you're ready to be promoted. But showing you can handle aspects of the job above you sure does, and that gets noticed."

Every company handles promotions differently. Some have strict policies about when they are given and what benchmarks you have to achieve. Find out from your boss or human resources department what the policy is and prepare your case accordingly.

Give specific examples of how you are already working at a higher level and, if you can, demonstrate how having a better title is going to help you do your job better and benefit the company. Make sure there is a precedent for your new title. At Calphalon Corporation, "director" positions don't exist and the managers are limited in their options for promotion. Do your homework on the policies and be prepared to make a compelling case if there is no precedent.

could i have more freedom?

If the ability to have a more flexible work schedule is an important job requirement, then you are among the hundreds of thousands of Americans who put it at the top of their list. You have a few options when considering a change in your job structure.

OPTION ONE: FLEXTIME

What it is: Working 40+ hours a week but not the typical 9–5 schedule. Maybe you come in at 8 A.M. and leave at 4 P.M., making sure to spend the majority of your day with the rest of the staff.

Tips for asking: When you negotiate, be sure to address how coming and going at different times won't disrupt the team, how you are going to handle any crisis that arises during the business hours that you are not in the office, and how you are going to fit meetings and other responsibilities into your new schedule.

OPTION TWO: FLEXWEEK

What it is: You want to have longer days Monday–Thursday so you can have Fridays off.

Tips for asking: This is a very common request, especially when women return from maternity leave, because it seems like the ideal work/life balance. Christine Deussen, founder of Deussen Global Communications, says that if approached by employees with this request, "I'd need reassurance that their team and clients would not suffer, that the company would not suffer, and in fact that the company would benefit."

OPTION THREE: TELECOMMUTING

What it is: Working from home some or all of the time.

Tips for asking: While the number of companies that offer this option is slowly growing, employees are wary of taking them up on it. Maybe it is the statistics that have shown that working from home part of the time can impact your job growth because of the overemphasis on face time, especially at the senior level. If this is something you want to ask for, then know that you will be facing skepticism about your commitment to the company. When positioning the request, keep it firmly focused on the benefits to the organization and how your increased flexibility will contribute to increased results. We suggest pointing out that by not commuting you can be at your desk earlier and leave later. Also, make it clear that you plan on spending time at the office, and will be accessible.

THE GOOD, BAD, AND UGLY ABOUT A FLEXIBLE WORK SCHEDULE

While it may seem like a huge quality-of-life upgrade to have a schedule that works around your personal responsibilities, you should go into it with your eyes open.

Good: You will be able to fit your work around your life, ideally creating more balance.

Bad: It may be hard for you to stick to the schedule during busy times, or when meetings are set during your off-hours.

Ugly: You may end up working much more than you were before, because you will likely have to be accessible during business hours. If you don't have a BlackBerry now, you will soon!

could i have another set of hands?

Before asking for more staff, even if it is a temp or part-timer, think through exactly what you want this new person to do. Most important, prepare to answer what this person will do to make the company better. Christine Deussen shares this: "If someone wants additional support staff, I'd like them to come to me with their reasons why, which should be based on a bottom-line benefit to the company. For example, I need to understand exactly why they need help, and exactly how the hire would benefit the company."

The more you think through this position, the better the meeting with your boss will go. Draft out a job description and be ready to explain exactly what this person will do and how their job can't be done by the existing staff. Plan ahead and figure out if there is a job they can grow into. Ask yourself if you can get away with hiring a part-time person instead, because the lower salary and no benefits will make it an easier sell. If the work you do is seasonal, then hiring a temp could get you through.

Remember that hiring an employee is an expensive proposition. The training of the newbie costs the company money, the salary and the benefits, the office equipment—all cost money. Think twice before asking for more staff if you want an assistant simply because you are tired of coordinating your own schedule or a new sales associate because you are bored with the long-distance sales calls. Go ahead and ask if you need an assistant because you're spending your valuable time on filing instead of the work that needs doing for your rapidly expanding portfolio. The only real reason a company will give you another set of hands is to help them make more money. If in focusing your time on the big stuff you will help them make more money, then it is tough to argue against your request.

could i have a day, a week, a month off?

In 2004, Salary.com conducted a survey that found that 39 percent of workers would take time off over the equivalent in additional base salary. If you want a day off or a vacation, the key to asking for time is making the request in advance. Make sure you are asking for days that you are entitled to, not an extra week. To make a great impression, set a time to meet with your boss the day before you leave to fill her in on the status of ongoing projects. We worked with someone who left for her honeymoon without doing this and almost lost her job because her team had no idea what was going on with her workload and wasted days trying to sort everything out.

VACATIONS DON'T CARRY OVER
We've gotten busier at work each year. Recently we increased the billings, added staff, secured another book contract, and developed a Web site—all at the same time. We realized that in the fourth quarter of last year, we worked forty-five straight days. And when we weren't

physically at work, we were worrying about it and frantically typing into our BlackBerrys. At some point, the wheels started to fall off. We were tired and cranky and it began to show in our work. We began to snipe at each other and the staff, and one day it got so bad that Kim started yelling at a client. Whoa. That's not good for business—we needed a fix and found it in the most obvious place, a vacation. How could we have forgotten? And truth be told, we probably would have forgotten if we hadn't returned from the Christmas holidays as completely different people—happier people—more like our old selves.

Industrial psychologists tell us that vacations are good for the bottom line, but not only do we forget, it seems corporate America does too. According to work habits surveys, the majority of people still take work with them on vacation in one form or another, and more than 25 percent of corporate people don't take any absolute downtime at all.

Skipping downtime acts a little like sleep deprivation, according to physicians and psychotherapists. Just as lack of sleep impedes your ability to think clearly and act decisively, lack of playtime keeps you from taking in information effectively and seeing the totality of a situation. Lack of sleep and play both have a negative impact on your reflex time, general resilience, and ability to ward off infection. Recreation deprivation also makes you cranky, and often more than a little critical of the people in your organization who do have the good sense to take care of themselves.

Here are some tips for a work- and stress-free vacation:

- **Plan for it.** Organize your work so you are covered when you are gone. Let others in the organization know what's happening with your projects and delegate the authority to make the decisions in your absence. We're not living in Europe and you won't be gone for six weeks, so let people know that some things may need to wait until you return.

- **Enjoy it.** You earned the time. Don't spend it worrying about what's going on in your absence. There will be plenty of time for that when you return.
- **Make it easy and take it easy.** Sure, you've always wanted to climb Machu Picchu, but is taking a long flight, twelve ground transfers, and altitude sickness really what you need right now? Consider what you really have the energy for and plan accordingly.

things you might not think to ask for

Don't forget that besides the old standbys (raises and promotions) there are a bunch of other job-enhancing benefits that you could ask for, including online courses; membership in professional organizations; corporate coaching; workshops on management; or classes to develop skills in language or computer programming.

when the answer is "no"

You won't always hear the answer you want. No matter how much you prepared or how much you deserve it, sometimes you will be turned down. There are some no's that you can live with and there are some no's that you can't. There are also some no's that are actually openings to a negotiation.

NO'S YOU CAN LIVE WITH

Shake it off and move on. Maybe the timing wasn't right. Maybe your request was poorly presented. Maybe they just didn't see the value of your request. Lynn Sherman was turned down for a request for a windowed office. Sure, it stung for a week or so, but she liked what she did enough for her to get over it. Lynn says, "I have even grown to like the quiet, OK cavelike, peace of my interior office." If it was something that you can live with not having, and you like your job enough to stay, then move on.

NO'S YOU CAN'T LIVE WITH

These are the no's that can change the direction of your life. Regina Lawrence thought she was doing an amazing job at her bank, and maybe she was, but when she asked for a promotion they said no.

> First, I got angry. Then, I had a choice to make: do I become resent-ful, pity-seeking, and walk around with a long face all day? Or do I regroup and become CEO of Me? I gave myself that title, and made every choice from that perspective. First, I realized that the depart-ment heads who were getting promotions were in areas more val-ued by the company, so I needed to expand my knowledge and responsibilities into areas that garnered more respect. I took classes (which the company paid for through their tuition reim-bursement program), and I refocused my work into doing more projects that were high profile. Not too long after channeling my energy from angry to focused productivity (instead of resentment), I was offered a great job at another company with a higher title and salary than the one I had been denied.

NO'S THAT ARE OPENINGS TO A NEGOTIATION

If you have been turned down for something but know you are valu-able to the company, and are liked by your boss, then try asking for something else, or some version of your original request. If you asked for a promotion and were turned down because there wasn't a position, then ask for a raise. If you asked for a raise and they said no, then ask for extra vacation time. If you asked for an office and were shut out, then ask for a small budget to redecorate. Pursue other requests only when the first "no" was not based in merit but in bureaucracy. Some yeses are just easier for companies to give.

At the very least when turned down, ask if you can revisit the topic in six months. Set performance goals with your boss for the follow-up meeting; use this as an opportunity to demonstrate your commitment to the company.

girl taking charge

We spoke to Kathleen Miller, founder of Snow Cabin Goods, an importer of hand-framed sweaters and a humanitarian about what she learned when she faced down her fear of asking.

Did you have a difficult time asking for what you needed from vendors?
Asking for anything is often challenging, particularly when it has to do with how others will perceive me. I am quite sensitive, self-conscious, and interested in pleasing others. So, I have to give myself a pep talk when I want to make difficult requests of others.

Was there a time you asked for what you needed and were really happy you did?
There were many times when even though I was scared, I asked for what I needed and was thrilled and surprised by how it was rewarded. One of the most pivotal experiences was at the very start of my business. I had traveled abroad to a trade show to scout around for sources. I really wanted to do business internationally, but I didn't have a track record or personal connections. After milling about for several hours, I asked one vendor at the show if they would take a chance and give me exclusive distribution to their line in North America. I was astonished that they agreed to the idea. I didn't realize it at the time, but they needed me, too. After I asked the first vendor, it was easier to ask the second and so on. Had I recoiled to the

safety of the familiar, I would not have developed some of the strongest business relationships that I now enjoy.

So what would you say to those of us who are challenged by having to ask for something?
Dig deep inside yourself and do things that make you feel good about yourself. In turn, you will build self-confidence and self-esteem. If you believe in yourself and take an active role in determining what makes you function at your best, you will be better equipped to put yourself out on a limb. You will be better able to get what you need, when you need it. Alternatively, you will be better able to handle the disappointments that will most certainly come your way.

a view from the ladder

We spoke to Linda Brierty, author of *The Self-Inquiry Process*, about why women shy away from asking for anything at work. She shared this invaluable advice.

Why don't women ask for what they need in the workplace?
Many women may have been socially conditioned not to make waves or rock the boat. If we go out on a limb by asking for something for ourselves, we may feel or appear aggressive. We need to ask ourselves if there is anything wrong with that. It is interesting to observe how often women will go to bat for someone else. I often suggest that women treat themselves as they would someone else; what would they tell a friend to do? Women historically have also been conditioned to play a supportive and at times a dependent role. We may have inherited certain belief systems. Self-esteem plays a part as well; some women do not feel that they deserve to move up. The flip side of that, which none of us may want to look at, is that we may be more comfortable being stuck and complaining about it. Beware the victim archetype.

Some women may wait to see what they are given at work. Ask yourself if you are being passive, aggressive, or assertive in the workplace. It takes intitiative and courage to speak up for yourself. It may feel like a risk. We may have deep-seated security issues that cause us to cling to situations out of fear. If we can strengthen our resolve to be on our own side, we will be fortified to get what we want. If we are not given it in one workplace, it may be a signal that it is time to move on. Don't accept the glass ceiling! Acknowledge that we all have some fear of change, yet change is inevitable. Try to see change as growth. Stagnation is not good for the soul. We may also have become used to certain patriarchal structures, and unwittingly accept them without challenging them. We bring our family and individual backgrounds into the workplace as well. Think of yourself as a role model for yourself and other women. Explore any fear of authority you may have and become the authority figure in your own life!

What is your advice to women struggling with this?
Summon up your innate potential of courage and take care of yourself. You will be proud of yourself for asking, regardless of the outcome—which you can't control. Don't personalize it if the answer is no. Don't give up—ask again or call that headhunter. Don't take no for the permanent answer. Don't settle. It is still a fight for equality out there, and a bit of a jungle. We need tactics that are appropriate for that reality. Being nice and submissive all the time may not be adaptive for getting ahead in the workplace. Become comfortable with competition—there is a way to compete in a positive and healthy way. Break any old labels that you are applying to yourself that may be standing in your way. We often stereotype ourselves and hold ourselves back. Remember, if you are not getting what you deserve, you need to ask yourself why that is. It is too easy to blame an external oppressor. Decide to have the victory and you will emerge stronger. Check to see if you are punishing yourself in any way. No one else will advocate for you the way you will. Choose to live a self-directed life, free from resentment. As you move up, you will also have to become more comfortable with others resenting your success. Ask your-

self if you are afraid of success or failure, or both . . . then go beyond fear.

What are your tips for asking for what you need, deserve?
When asking for what you need or deserve, be professional. Keep your emotions out of it. Be prepared by making a nonconfrontational case for yourself, a list of reasons why you are asking. Make a proposal of what would make your situation better. Don't rely on your employer to notice you or chart your course for you. Be creative and create the best scenario for yourself. Think like a businessperson. Why would what you are asking for also benefit the business? Also, keep your options open in the marketplace. Women tend to be loyal, sometimes to their own detriment. Get another offer and negotiate. Isn't this what men do? Learn to sell yourself—humility can be overrated in the workplace. Ask for a meeting and bring your agenda. You may also have to follow up on the discussion. Keep the energy positive; it achieves more than negative energy does.

What is the source of this "asking" insecurity?
When we are asking, we are making ourselves vulnerable and opening ourselves up for possible rejection—if we interpret it that way. Sometimes it feels easier to hide or fly under the radar. We are also close to our emotions, and it can be more difficult to maintain that thick skin in business. Being a woman in business requires a set of skills to cultivate: resilience, strength, the ability to be tough when necessary, the ability to put emotions to the side, and not acting out of fear. A common trap is for women to fall into the overworking, overhelping syndrome and then feel taken advantage of and unappreciated. We are responsible for getting our needs met. We are afraid to ask when we think that someone has power over us. We may have a fear that we will be punished for being assertive, or even successful. Sadly, this is sometimes the case. The first step is asking ourselves what we want and need, then translating that into action.

eleven

chick in charge (leadership, management, and the fine art of delegating)

Are you the woman who feels more comfortable doing it herself? Can't let go and delegate? You're worried you'll hurt someone's feelings when you offer constructive criticism. You want to be everybody's friend. Don't worry, you're not alone. These are common pitfalls female leaders fall into—and we're going to show you how to avoid them. Even if you choose (as we did) to work with a small team, you need leadership skills. This chapter explores those pesky and often problematic leadership qualities: "team-building," "inspiring," "problem-solving," "influencing upward," and "delegating." These are the skills that are going to set you apart from the competition and help you move up in your job or be successful in a new venture. Trying to do everything yourself will only hold you back.

When surveyed, men and women senior managers gave high marks to women leaders on the stereotypically feminine skills of "supporting," "rewarding," "mentoring," "networking," and "consulting," so we won't focus on them here. We girls don't fare nearly as well when it comes to those stereotypically "masculine" skills. The bad rap goes like this: women don't build and lead effective *teams*. Women aren't as *inspiring* as men. We're weak on *influencing upward*. We can't let go, so we don't *delegate* effectively.

While you may feel in control when trying to control everything, we promise you, your life will be a lot easier if you start using the strengths of the people around you. This chapter will be a management primer—everything you need to know about how to run the show.

we know: "there's no 'i' in team"

A team is a group organized to work together to accomplish a set of objectives that cannot be achieved effectively by any one individual. It seems simple enough—it takes a village, after all. But how do you get people working well together when it's hard enough getting them to work well on their own?

Susan Heathfield, a human resources columnist for www.about .com and a management and organizational development consultant with more than thirty years' experience, has helped organizations of all shapes and sizes increase team performance. She shared her "12 C's for Effective Team-Building" with us.

- **Clear Expectations:** Has executive leadership clearly communicated its expectations for the team's performance and expected outcomes? Do team members understand why the team was created?
- **Context:** Do team members understand why they are participating on the team? Do they understand how the strategy of

using teams will help the organization attain its communicated business goals?

- **Commitment:** Do team members want to participate on the team? Do team members feel the team mission is important? Do team members perceive their service as valuable to the organization and to their own careers?
- **Competence:** Are the right people on the team? Does the team feel that its members have the knowledge, skill, and capability to address the issues for which the team was formed?
- **Charter:** Has the team taken its assigned area of responsibility and designed its own mission, vision, and strategies to accomplish the mission?
- **Control:** Does the team have enough freedom and empowerment to feel the ownership necessary to accomplish its charter? At the same time, do team members clearly understand their boundaries? Is the team's reporting relationship and accountability understood by all members of the organization?
- **Collaboration:** Does the team understand team and group process? Are team members working together effectively interpersonally? Do all team members understand the roles and responsibilities of team members?
- **Communication:** Are team members clear about the priority of their tasks? Is there an established method for the teams to give feedback and receive honest performance feedback?
- **Creative Innovation:** Is the organization really interested in change? Does it value creative thinking, unique solutions, and new ideas? Does it reward people who take reasonable risks to make improvements?
- **Consequences:** Do team members feel responsible and accountable for team achievements? Are rewards and recognition supplied when teams are successful?
- **Coordination:** Are teams coordinated by a central leadership

team that assists the groups to obtain what they need for success? Have priorities and resource allocation been planned across departments?

- **Cultural Change:** Does the organization recognize that the team-based, collaborative, empowering, enabling organizational culture of the future is different from the traditional, hierarchical organization it may currently be?

a problem by any other name . . . is an opportunity

In our professional lives, we're faced with challenges each and every day. They range from the mundane to the absolutely mind-boggling. When we're short on time or stressed out (which is usual), even the mundane seems overwhelming. But it doesn't have to. Strong leaders make good decisions—they have a process that helps them achieve a good outcome. We're going to share our process with you, but we also offer a note of caution. We've turned many a small challenge into major crisis by voicing our anxieties. If you are faced with a challenge and you're handling it, then nine times out of ten you should keep it to yourself.

Problem-solvers are the most valuable resources in an organization. It's too easy for staff members to bring their problems to their managers. We've instituted a policy whereby our senior staff must come to us with solutions or at the very least recommendations before we will engage. Experience is the only way you'll learn, and if you never solve your own problems, you won't gain experience and you won't move up.

We've found that, sometimes, the biggest problems are the ones that upset us the least—because we have no control over them—and the little ones are the ones that suck up all our energy. When our attorney filed our trademark papers incorrectly for the Girl's Guide, we didn't know for six months. By the time we learned of the mistake, the attorney had refiled the petition correctly and there was nothing we could do but wait and see if it was going to be a problem. Potentially, this could have been a disaster, cost us thousands of dollars, and crippled our business, but since there was nothing we could do to fix it, we had no other option but to wait and see and get ourselves prepared for the worst.

We immediately consulted another attorney about the ramifications of the mistake. We made sure to get proof in writing that it was rectified, and we documented every call, printed our e-mail trail, and waited.

First step: identify what the actual problem is. Do some research and gather all of the facts—no matter how long it takes—before you snap to judgment, place blame, or panic. If you're faced with a complex problem that seems overwhelming even after some initial fact-finding, then see if you can break it down into smaller problems. If the problem isn't confidential, by all means seek outside resources.

Try to gather all the facts you know about the problem and write them down. It's a good habit to get into, because if the issue generates legal ramifications, it's important to have everything documented. If you discover several related problems, then set some priorities for dealing with them. Make sure you objectively address your role in the situation. Our research has shown that when women make mistakes they feel so guilty about their role that they spend more time beating themselves up than addressing the accountabilities of others or focusing on fixing the mistake.

Make sure you understand the causes of the problems and solicit as many views as possible before making a final judgment. If you're working as a group on the issue, then get them together and brainstorm some solutions. Work through a couple of different scenarios—you can even role-play difficult conversations.

Choose a solution that best solves the problem in the short and long term. If the solution requires money, evaluate the resources you have available. Many problems are easily solved by throwing money at them—pay a triple rush charge, overnight fees, overtime—but those solutions won't prevent the problem from happening again. If there was a failure in a system, make sure to fix the system and not just the problem.

We had a situation with a client recently where the simple writing of a press release had become a tortuous and time-consuming back and forth. In the public relations business, time is money, so we told the client that we wouldn't write the releases anymore—they would have to send us an outline and we would take it from there. The client suggested an easier and more service-friendly solution—have a brainstorm session at the beginning of every release process so that we're in agreement on the priorities and messaging before we begin. Wish we had thought of that.

When you have a solution, move forward and watch it each step of the way to make sure it's working the way it was intended. And then follow up and close the loop. It could be as simple as sending an e-mail to everyone involved letting them know of a new system.

delegate, don't dump

Delegating, not dumping, is the advice all management books will give you. But what does that really mean? If you pass along your work to your staff, aren't you by nature dumping it on them? Not at all. Delegating appropriately frees a manager's time to focus on other challenges while giving the staff opportunities to increase their responsibilities, grow, and learn.

As the manager responsible for the bigger picture, you should have identified all the goals your organization needs to accomplish and by when. You know the talents and resources that your staff (and you) offer. Delegating is the process of matching up the tasks with the best resources (your team members) to accomplish your goals.

Delegating effectively begins with communication. Communicate the bigger goal. Communicate how the person's unique talents make them the perfect person for the job. Communicate to them how taking on this task or new responsibility will help them grow. Communicate when you need the job done. And most important, communicate that while you will be there every step of the way to support them, this is now their responsibility and you trust them to use their creativity and energy to get it done.

Delegating requires trust. A manager trusts a subordinate with an important task (or project) and the subordinate trusts that the manager will support her through the process and reward her for good work.

The hardest part for the manager is managing resources. We never feel we have anyone to delegate to. Our small team is maxed out—which means somewhere in the process we mismanaged. Should we have charged more in the beginning so we could afford to bring on more resources? Is there something in our process that is slowing everyone down? Are people not working effectively or smartly enough? Answering these questions will be the key to our success and yours. Make sure you're always thinking about the best way to utilize the resources that you have.

DELEGATING MEANS

You have more time to:
- focus on the important things;
- network;
- think big picture;
- work on long-term planning; and

champion the accomplishments of your team to those above you.

Your team:
- gets more responsibility;
- learns new skills;
- gains your trust; and
- gets promoted and passes their lessons down to their team.

HOW TO GET THE MOST FROM YOUR REPORTS

Before Tiscia Eicher left her role as vice president of marketing at the Calphalon Corporation to take a year off, we asked her to share her tips for getting the best work from the team.

- Get team members what they need and never slow anyone down. My top priority is to get my team what they need so they can keep making progress without me. Only then do I get my own stuff done.
- Capitalize on how my team members are different from me. Hire people who know loads of stuff I don't know and ask them to teach me.
- "Train" team members through relevant projects, assignments, and experiences. Rarely are formal classes as effective.
- Create a "routine" team members can count on. Chaos or inconsistency can be exhausting and distracting. Stick to commitments for routine one-to-one discussions, monthly staff meetings to share results, sales calls, or whatever's relevant to that work environment. They need to know they can count on a few sacred opportunities each week/month to be heard, whether it's to share news, ask questions, get direc-

tion, voice concerns, share in successes, resolve issues, etc., in the midst of what's always a hectic environment.

- Manically keep team members focused on the stuff that really drives the business. Try to take all the other stuff off their plates, no matter how much they seem to be drawn to it.

DIRTY LITTLE SECRET: WE LOVE A BUSINESS TRIP

We were on a business trip with some other working mothers in Toledo and stayed at a less-than-fancy hotel. We got into our rooms before a dinner meeting, checked some e-mails, took a shower, watched some television—in short, relaxed—and it felt great. When we got to dinner and began to chat with the others, it turns out that they had done exactly the same thing! We're definitely on to something. For working mothers, business trips are a luxury and we enjoy them. When we're at home, our time is spoken for 100 percent of the time. When we're on the road, and we've finished the workday, no responsibilities await us and we make the most of it. Sometimes we exercise. Sometimes we get an extra hour of sleep, and sometimes, when we're feeling really naughty, we order hot fudge sundaes from room service.

THE GIRL'S GUIDE TOKEN BOY TAKING CHARGE

The great thing about the business world is it changes so quickly. The terrifying thing about the business world is it changes so quickly. Today's hot idea might not be tomorrow's. But there are greater guiding principles we can follow to help us navigate our careers. And we've sought out one of our favorite boys to share some guidance with us.

At first glance, he seems young to be so wise, but make no mistake, Bill Mehleisen is more than a pretty face. At thirty-one, he's a retired hedge fund manager and on a quest for the next "big" thing. After graduating from Union College in upstate New York, he took the traditional route, first working as a consultant for Anderson Consulting (at the time, a big eight consulting and accounting firm) and then moved to Wall Street to become a bond trader for Deutsche Bank. He loved the bond market, because even though everyone knew the game was about making the most money possible, the market operated on a serious framework of trust. Multimillion-dollar deals were done with a phone call. It was an industry where your word was literally your bond. At Deutsche Bank, he hooked up with a group of like-minded fellows and they decided to try their luck starting up their own internal prop trading fund (a lot like a hedge fund) for Credit Lyonnais in London. After a successful run, Bill and one of his partners decided to give up the world of finance and go in search of meaning in the entrepreneurial world and began studying with esteemed management guru, Marshall Thurber. We met Bill at a leadership conference and were so impressed by his outlook on business and his desire to bring people together to do great things that we were compelled to bestow the honor of "Token Male" on him and include his insights in this book.

What is the next thing?
We all know a great structural change has occurred. We may not think of it in those terms, but the Internet is a huge structural change. There is access to information about whatever you want, where and whenever you want it. It affects absolutely everything, and it means that the key to a business's success in the future will be integrity.

You lost us.
Look at it this way. If you are applying for a job now, the first thing a hiring manager will do is Google you and then they will move to MySpace, all in an effort to find out what you're really about. And

it's a virtuous system: the potential employee will be doing their homework too, trying to figure out if the sales pitch is true. If you try to misrepresent yourself in the interview and you have contradictory information on the Web, *somewhere*, somebody will find it.

Consider another example from traditional advertising. Let's say you see an ad for a car on television. Previously, you had to go to the dealership and be abused by the car salesman's pitch. Now, you'll immediately go to a community Web site with expertise in evaluating cars, such as Carmax, Car & Driver, Edmunds, or even Yahoo! or Google. On these sites, you get the real skinny from actual users about the quality of the car, and if the car you're investigating has terrible reviews, you probably won't buy it. The missing piece: integrity. Sure, the carmaker got you interested in the car with their seductive advertising, but the community is telling you don't believe the hype. The carmaker's offer lacked integrity because their sales pitch wasn't congruent with the actual quality of their product, and they lose the sale before you ever set foot in a dealership. That car salesman doesn't even get the chance to "close" you because you've already rejected their offer. This old world model of advertising tells only the "official" carmaker story. For discerning customers, the community (that is, fellow car buyers) tells the real story. And with the explosion of the Internet and communication technology it is increasingly easier to get the real story for almost anything and thus absolutely essential to always act with integrity.

So whom should we look to to drive this integrity in business?
There are leaders emerging in business today who have a very good understanding of this integrity model. They are creating businesses and pushing organizations to behave differently. There are all kinds of different names and classifications for leaders. The term I like the most is evolutionary business leaders.

How does evolutionary leadership fit into the integrity picture?
An evolutionary leader has the ability to give a problem back to their community in a way that gets them to evolve to the best an-

swers for a given situation. An evolutionary leader is moving from the scarcity world of win-lose to the abundant world of win-win.

And what does *that* mean?
Evolutionary leaders want to create a profitable business that makes a difference for their community, families, customers, and employees. And the core theme is integrity and learning how to act with it consistently, because if you don't, you get found out in a hurry.

How do we act with integrity in business?
The easiest place to start is with authenticity. Look for congruence. I'm a math guy at heart and congruence always speaks to me. Congruence is defined as the quality or state of agreeing or correspondence, and it means be true to yourself and match your actions to the context of the situation. Remember when you were a child and your mother told you if anything ever feels "icky" to speak up? That "icky" feeling is the opposite of congruence. Trust your instincts.

What else should we know about evolutionary leaders?
Evolutionary leaders understand the difference between being a learner and being a knower. They are confident learners. They understand that asking the right question is often better than having the right answer. In my experience we are not trained this way. Our system of education trains us to be knowers and reinforces that behavior by constantly testing us on what we know rather than our ability to learn and ask questions. I've seen this play out in the business world. Managers (women and men alike) are often consumed with having the right answers because they believe that is what defines their value. So they spend their days telling people what to do and how to do it. However, in this day and age, information changes so quickly that often what you knew last week is no longer valid this week. Evolutionary leaders understand that their role is to give the problem back to the people they are leading. They ask questions of those people in order to help them find the answers and solve the problems. In this way they are

creating a space for people to evolve. In the process everyone learns more and is acknowledged for being part of the process. That is my understanding and experience of evolutionary leaders—leaders who have the ability to give a problem back to their community in a way that gets them to evolve to the best answers for a given situation.

So how do evolutionary leaders do this?
They come from a place of being interested and asking questions. And they create a network of experts who know more then they do in various domains. When they have a problem, they go to the appropriate expert for advice and perspective. Then the process is pretty simple: ask questions, listen, consolidate the opinions, consider the options, and then have the courage to make a decision knowing you may make a mistake. Evolutionary leaders expect to make mistakes because they are just part of the process. They embrace mistakes as learning experiences and quickly course correct.

FIFTEEN THINGS WE LEARNED FROM GIRLS TAKING CHARGE

After finishing up this book we reread all of our Girls Taking Charge interviews and created this list of the top fifteen things we learned from the women we spoke to. We were inspired by every story and piece of advice, and we hope you were too. We won't be offended if you rip this list out and stick it near your computer for a daily reminder of how great it feels to take charge.

1. Believe in yourself.
2. Don't listen to anyone discouraging you from reaching your goal.
3. Know where you want to take yourself.

4. Don't lose your sense of humor.
5. Don't be threatened by a colleague's success. Be inspired by it.
6. Don't assume people are noticing your accomplishments.
7. Embrace your unique professional style.
8. Know what is important to you in life as well as in work.
9. Find something you are passionate about.
10. Define your own success.
11. Give back by mentoring someone.
12. Share your stories with other women.
13. Respect the input and ideas of others.
14. Look for a mentor who knows more than you do.
15. See women's differences as professional strengths, not weaknesses.

a view from the ladder

Whenever we're feeling overwhelmed with work we call Chrisi Colabella for advice and the first question she asks is, "What are you going to give away?" Chrisi is a master of delegation and she's the perfect girl to interview about management. But since we had already tapped her wisdom on selling, she volunteered to delegate the interview to her vice president of operations, Charlene Sperger. Perfect.

Charlene Sperger was recently promoted to vice president of operations at Construction Information Systems. She's been an operations manager for seven years. She joined CIS after a seventeen-year hiatus from the workforce while she stayed home to raise her three children. She started as a part-time research reporter and was the sixth person hired at the company. During her eleven-year tenure, she has worked every job in operations. She fosters a collaborative environment, holds her people to high standards, and delegates responsibility whenever possible. She shares her secrets for hiring good people and motivating them to grow within the company.

As the company grew, how did you identify the right people to hire?

I have worked every position in Operations, so I know which skill set each requires. As we started to grow and hire more people, I looked for people who could work well together as a team, projected positive energy and enthusiasm, and would help the company grow.

Do you have a management philosophy?

When Chrisi first asked me to supervise new employees, the only relevant experience I had had was running my house. I was at my best when every member of the family had a role in the chores and was accountable to the household. Whenever I handled the whole house myself, I lost energy and got bored and we all would suffer. I look at my role in the company the same way. If I do everything myself, then the whole company will suffer—everyone has to do their part to end up with the most efficient house on the block.

I try to see what motivates my staff as individuals and in groups. I manage three internal and one external department. The great thing about CIS is that there is tremendous room for growth, and I use that as a motivator for my top performers. It hit home when Chrisi used the same philosophy on me, so I knew I had to pass it on.

All of my people like to be appreciated when they make an extra effort or do extraordinary work, and they should be. So I've implemented a rewards system. It's easy to administer, costs the company very little money, and keeps morale high. If I notice (or better, when a supervisor makes me aware) that someone is going above and beyond, staying late or coming in early, or helping other members of their team, then I will reward them with a gift certificate to Borders as one example. I have a person whose favorite color is yellow. She had been working very hard, so one day I bought her a bouquet of yellow daffodils. She was thrilled. It was a very small gesture for me but made a big difference to her.

How do you hold people accountable?

CIS is a leads service, and my teams are responsible for collecting the leads and entering them into the database—every day. We're only as good as our information, and if our information is faulty or not in the system by the end of the day, then we will have unhappy customers. I make sure everyone understands how important their role is to our customers, and if they miss deadlines or are sloppy, then the entire company suffers. I make sure that everybody feels respected, recognized, and rewarded by their management.

What techniques do you use to get people back on track?

Communication is key. We have a lot of meetings where I have to do a lot of listening. If I see things that I want my supervisors to do differently, we'll talk through the situations and explore different options for handling them. I will share the benefit of my experience, but I give my senior people the time and counsel so they believe they are initiating the change. Sometimes we role-play if it's a difficult situation. But ultimately, I try to give them the tools and authority to come up with a solution, even if I knew the answer all along.

When we have little meetings because someone is not performing well, I make sure that the supervisor has been seeing and keeping track of things along the way. We work with people from day one on. When they really aren't getting it but showing an attitude that they want to be counted on to get certain duties accomplished, we review expectations and try to discover where they need extra help. When all of that fails, we have to replace them with better employees.

What are your biggest management challenges?

In the short term, my biggest challenge is to never miss a beat. I need to keep the successful people happy in their positions, stay ahead of our competition, keep the communication going, and work daily as a team.

In the long term, I am working to find ways that the company can grow—whether we expand into new territories or new product offerings.

girl taking charge

As host of About.com's human resources site since 2000, management guru Susan Heathfield gets inundated with interview requests. We were thrilled when she agreed to share her thoughts about women, leadership, and empowering employees. Luckily for us, she shared more insight and advice than we could have hoped for. Susan is one of those girls who has seen enough to know what works and isn't afraid to tell it like it is. She's a true fiscal conservative who believes in small government and low taxation. She also believes that people are competent, capable, and able to make their own way in the world with little interference.

Susan started her career in the early 1970s as a high school special education and English teacher. She realized pretty quickly that her chosen profession was going to "bore her out of her skull." She loved the kids but didn't love the environment and moved out of teaching and into adult education, where she managed the largest community college extension center in Michigan.

After ten years of running the center, she was ready for her next challenge. As a matter of fact, at thirty-four years old she was ready for a complete career change. The head of one of her doctoral committees called her at home one morning and told her he had found her next career, a four-year contract job in management development and training at a General Motors plant in Lansing, Michigan. That's where Susan got her start in manufacturing, the almost exclusively male industry that defined her career for the next twenty years.

After her contract with GM ended, the only job available to her was a ninety-minute commute away. Unable to make that lifestyle choice and unwilling to leave her future in the hands of another big company, Susan began interviewing locally. She quickly realized she was overqualified for most of the jobs she was being interviewed for, as did her potential employers. A few of them recognized what she had to offer and hired her to do contract projects, and soon her consulting practice was launched.

Susan spent half her time working as a consultant for Michigan Modernization Service, a state agency dedicated to helping small- to mid-size manufacturing companies modernize. While under contract she traveled around the state with a representative from the client and made recommendations to various manufacturing companies on how they could update and improve their organizational and human resources systems.

While with Michigan Modernization Service, she worked directly with more than fifty-five companies over the course of four years and realized that she could have a very lucrative future in consulting because all of these companies lacked a strategic vision and had no systems in place to energize and empower their workforce. While meeting with the various companies, she was often the only woman in the room yet had very little problem getting heard because she always had confidence, conviction, and a proven track record of success.

She visited many companies preaching that their employees were their most important assets, yet she saw very few that actually instituted any changes based on her recommendations.

How do you put "actions behind the words" and empower your employees?

I think it's pretty easy if you make it a priority. My husband started a software company in 1987 that now boasts 170 employees. We live what I preach on my Web site. For example, we are building a new facility for the company. We've hired architects and space designers to interview and survey every single staff member about their space needs and what kind of workplace environment they will be most productive in.

Sure, an executive committee will make the final decisions, but those decisions will be based on the input from the entire group.

In my consulting practice, I met managers who consistently preached the value of people but missed the essential point. I know I can adopt the technology of any company competing with me down the street, but I absolutely can't duplicate the workforce.

Talk to us about your experience with women in the workplace.

To this day, very few women work in senior management in the manufacturing industry—although there are many more in the pipeline and I am doing my best to champion their cause. For the most part, I have found that women do things that undermine their accomplishments and contributions.

Recently, a vice president at one of my clients called. He was confused because I put forth three excellent, prequalified female candidates for a leadership position in his company. He didn't know who to hire because, after interviewing each one of them individually, he had no idea what they had personally contributed to their past organizations. The women spoke about their accomplishments in terms of "we." We did this, we accomplished that, we succeeded in this, to the point where the hiring manager had no idea what the women had actually done as individuals.

But isn't that how we're supposed to be? Aren't managers supposed to speak in terms of their group's accomplishments and not their individual talents?

Sure, that's how it's supposed to be. But remember, we still are living in a world where men are in the positions of power, so women need to be savvier in dealing with them. Here's another example. A couple of years ago I was in a group of executives: one woman, five men, and I was the facilitator. I was working on team-building. As an icebreaker, I asked each of them to go around the room and introduce themselves. When it was the woman's turn to speak, she burst into tears while telling her story. She'd just been through a terrible breakup of her company and many people had lost their jobs. She was clearly still raw, and with good reason, but that display of emotion defined her to her colleagues and I am really not sure how it will affect her in the long term.

So what should women do?

I don't want women to be anything other than women, but it's important to recognize that men still occupy most of the positions of power. Look at the behaviors that you exhibit that may not be personally empowering. For a woman to come to a job interview and never once say "I did this" means that she is missing an opportunity to market herself and champion her accomplishments. While the world has not ever been as supportive of female leadership as I would like to see, I believe in personal responsibility, and women can change things.

Women possess all the skills to be great leaders. They just need to market them better.

I'd sure like to see more women mentoring women. Those of us who have developed successful careers have an obligation to mentor others, both women and men. There is so much you can teach someone starting their career. They are like sponges, and the smart young people can save themselves years of mistakes by developing relationships with savvy, experienced people.

a final note

When we sat down to write a new final note for the paperback edition, we were stumped. The economy had all but collapsed since we published the hardcover edition—how could we provide inspiration during these difficult times? We know how hard it is out there. Our public relations business, while still going, is tougher than it's ever been. Our clients want more for less (which we can handle) but because of *their* cash flow problems they are paying us sixty to ninety days late (which we absolutely cannot handle). We could be the poster children for the evil merry-go-round that small businesses are facing right now: one of our credit lines has been pulled and all of our clients are paying late, so we're forced to pay all of our vendors late, which undermines our credit, which will make it harder for us to get our credit line back when the banks start to release money again.

All of these changes at work have forced us to make changes at home, too. Caitlin has moved her family to Brooklyn and added a two-hour commute to her day so the twins can go to a great public school. Kim has been forced to look at all of her expenses and cut everything that is not absolutely necessary. Her lack of cushion (which in the good times never seemed important) has forced her to cut back on all nonessential items. Gone are dining out multiple times a week, clothes shopping, fancy vacations, and even the consideration of sending her son to private school for fourth grade. She's also been getting regular calls from collection agents because of payments that are merely two days past due.

The funny thing about all of this, though, is that when we were forced to sit down and look at the past year and all of the struggles and changes (and downsizing) we've gone through, we realized it really hasn't been that bad. And more importantly, we've relied on our strengths and strategies to maintain our equilibrium, as well as the network that we've nurtured over the past twenty years, which has really come through for us. By employing the lessons in this book (we practice what we preach!), we've managed to not only remain in business but we now also have the confidence to handle anything that will come our way in the future.

While this is no small lesson to be reminded of in difficult times, still we wanted to offer readers more in this "A Final Note"—we wanted to commiserate with you, cheer you on, and offer the right advice, in just a few pages. When we called our editor to voice our challenges and frustrations, she told us the most obvious thing in the world: "Seek out women who have been affected by the recession and share their stories. Share the lessons."

Of course. Do what we do best. Share the stories. And we've got many. Once the financial news started to get bad, our phones began ringing with requests from former colleagues who were worried about their jobs or who had been laid off. And when we put the call out for stories through Facebook and LinkedIn, more just kept coming. Women may be losing their jobs at a slightly slower pace then men, but for a while it seemed as if every single day someone we knew had lost their job. We were giving out advice, reviewing résumés, and passing names along like crazy.

One woman who came to us was Sumika Badj. Prior to the "Great Recession," Sumika was an account executive at a small public relations firm in New York City, where she managed a portfolio of food, beverage, and luxury lifestyle clients. At the beginning of May 2009, her employer warned the team that clients might be leaving or not renewing and that changes would be made accordingly. Sumika estimated she'd be out of a job at the end of the summer and started getting her résumé in order. Just two weeks later, all of her clients left the agency—not even finishing out their contracts—and she (along with a few other employees) was laid off.

Sumika immediately went to her network and told everyone she knew and asked them to let everyone they knew know that she was on the job hunt, and that's how she came to us. We reviewed her résumé and suggested a number of ways to frame her accomplishments more strongly and directly. (Common mistake alert: avoid jargon, boilerplate, and sweeping generalizations in résumés. Be specific and use numbers to illustrate success stories where possible. See Chapter Two.)

After six weeks, seven interviews for open positions, and countless "informationals," Sumika still hadn't landed a full-time position. She has terrific work experience, excellent references, and isn't too expensive, so she should be doing better than 0–7. It was time for an in-person session to see whether her interview skills needed a polish. After about a minute of conversation we identified what was going wrong. Sumika was simply not selling her accomplishments or positioning herself as a "driver" even though all of the work she had done (when you pulled it out of her) exemplified "driver" behaviors. When asked what her busiest days were, she answered, "the day of events." Now everyone in the PR industry knows what event days are like, but Sumika's potential employer needs her to demonstrate what her version of events days was like and what her role and responsibilites on those days were. Once we pressed her for further details, she told us story after story that made us wish we could offer her a position on the spot. This was a girl who knew her stuff, who worked hard and strategically, and who really loved what she did. The problem was that you wouldn't have ever guessed that until you pressed her.

And it's not just Sumika. We've counseled at least twenty women who are making the exact same mistake. Whether they aren't comfortable bragging about their successes or really don't know how to sell themselves well, we're not sure. But Sumika's story underscores an important lesson. In this incredibly competitive environment, we have to sell ourselves more aggressively and effectively than ever.

Another one of our favorite girls, Holly Bohn, founder of See Jane Work (www.seejanework.com) shared with us how she is surviving and thriving ITE, and we want to share it as a bonus "View from the Ladder."

a view from the ladder

Tell us about your business before the Great Recession?

Before the recession business was growing rapidly at a 500 percent compound annual growth. It was easy to get the necessary capital to fuel that level of growth. It was a fun and exciting time. That's not to say there weren't challenges. Every business owner has struggles, even when the economy is good.

How has the economy impacted your business?

The economy changed my business overnight. Surprisingly, the biggest challenge was not reduced sales, although there were some of those, but my problem became raising capital. If I had been through this before I probably would have been a bit more prepared and taken corrective measures sooner, however, I just didn't know it would get this bad this quickly. First, the banks closed our credit lines, and then vendors, facing the same action from their banks, switched to prepayment terms. This meant that any inventory purchases would need to be paid for 100 percent up front. Customers wanted to buy product, but where would I get the money to buy the inventory? Investors were scared and broke from the stock market decline, so no one was interested or had additional money to gamble and invest in a retail company.

At the same time, vendors were going out of business, leaving us with no product to sell even when we had them featured in magazines. As there was no way to correct this due to magazine lead times, when a magazine hit the stands featuring one of our products, we couldn't ship, creating unsatisfied customers. And, even when we could still buy the product from a vendor, we still didn't have the cash to pay for it (see original problem).

If that wasn't bad enough, the inventory situation reduced our sales level while our FedEx and UPS rates increased. The rates had been increased in 2008 when oil prices went up, but when the oil prices came back down, shipping rates didn't follow. I spoke with larger retailers who didn't suffer the same fate. Small business just doesn't have enough power to negotiate better terms like the big guys.

How have you adjusted your business because of the new economic realities?

I have gotten very creative. We tried two different joint ventures, but both of those companies were taken over by the banks and they evaporated. We requested help from the SBA, but they said that there weren't provisions in the stimulus package for retailers like us.

I then sought out businesses that had different challenges than ours. Despite a few bad experiences, I have continued with joint ventures. It allows you to partner with someone who has complementary strengths and weaknesses.

We have cut back staff and many other monthly expenses. This has been a positive experience though. It is amazing how much you can do without when forced. I had some staff who actually asked for more money despite the economic downturn. They told me the company wouldn't make it without them, but we have! I just wish I had made some of these changes sooner. Positive cash flow can lull you into complacency.

I've also been amazed at the anger. Everyone seems so angry. I'm much more likely to help someone or direct any cash flow I have to employees or vendors who have a positive attitude. I don't need more stress. I want to work with people who can cope with the changes.

What personal adjustments have you had to make?

My life has completely changed. I haven't been paid in more than five months and my savings is gone. I've actually started clipping coupons again, something I haven't done since college. My home is at risk. It's very scary. No one knows how much worse things will get. The stress of my home keeps me awake at night. My children missed all sports programs last year, even tutoring became too expensive. We don't eat out, buy clothes or video games, etc.

Have the changes had a positive effect on any part of your life? On the way you do things, think about things?

I don't regret the changes for a moment. First of all, my faith in God has been strengthened. That alone gives me a lot of peace. I also now see myself as a survivor. I didn't grow up in a wealthy family. I often felt a bit resentful growing up as my friends had cars, clothes, and spending money. Now that I'm going through these difficulties I see that I was actually blessed. My friends who grew up with money are far more upset about current circumstances than I am. I've been without before, and I can handle it.

I also see how much more I could have given of my time and resources when times were good. If I had done without some of the luxuries before the downturn, I could have directed that money to someone in need. I also see how much time I'm currently spending trying to keep the business growing. I could have spent that time before. I was happy with status quo, and I never want to live like that again.

All of these stories we've heard over the last year have led us to create a little list of "Five Lessons We Wish We Never Had to Learn from the Great Recession but Are Incredibly Useful Nonetheless."

1. Sell, sell, sell. You need to sell your accomplishments in the terms that your future (or current) employer wants to hear them. (Okay, we knew this one, but never is it a more important lesson to remember).
2. Money is tight. For everyone. Now is not the time to make financial demands. Showing how you can control costs, help the bottom line, and be a team player is the way to everyone's heart. When things get better, make your move. (You have been keeping track of all of your successes and sacrifices along the way, right?)
3. Bottom-line thinking and going without aren't as bad as you think. We won't pretend there isn't an adjustment period, but once you make it through, you are okay. (Kim still can't believe that she enjoys price-shopping. She never considered it worth her time before, but now she's renegotiated the phone plan at work, cut down her cable bill at home, and avidly compares rental car prices online—no more Hertz Gold Club for her; that name in lights thing has nothing on the feeling of an extra $150 in her pocket.)
4. Your network is the only capital you will be able to depend on. It's really about who you know. Relationships are key. There is a reason our phone started ringing off the hook when things got bad. We can help people find jobs. And we did. And when we need something, those same people will be there for us.
5. Flexibility is the key to success. If you are willing to think and work creatively, you will always be able to make a living. It might not be in the traditional job that you had before, but you can still make money. Don't rule anything out. Consider part-time positions, short-term projects, and even interning for free for a lit-

tle while to build relationships and skills. With the extensions to unemployment benefits (we know most people can't live on unemployment alone, and who wants to?) and a reduction in costs, you will find a way to hang on until something better comes along. Prior to "The Great Recession" Carolee Eubanks was a self-employed writer of search engine optimization (SEO) pages from home and was paid by the page. After the downturn, her primary customer cut back her work from "do as much work as you'd like" to "hit this much-smaller maximum target of pages per week." The result was a 75 percent drop in compensation. While she was "under-employed" (a very common problem that no one wants to talk about) and looking for work, Carolee took her extra time and home-schooled her children two days a week. When a temp-to-hire position came up, she lowered her normal hourly rate and loosened her restrictions on commuting. Going from a room-to-room commute to one that was an hour each way was not as traumatic as she expected. She learned to be satisfied with something other than the ideal. If she hadn't been forced to cut back on work, she wouldn't have had those months watching her kids learn and explore, and if she hadn't been flexible on the commute, she wouldn't have begun a new chapter in her career. She told us, "Everything has a way of turning out well if you allow it to have a bright side."

We couldn't agree more.

resources

CAREER ADVICE

- www.monster.com
- U.S. Bureau of Labor Statistics: www.bls.gov/oes
- *BusinessWeek*: www.businessweek.com
- Career Builder: www.careerbuilder.com
- The *Wall Street Journal* Executive Career Site: www.career journal.com

SUPPORT

- Catalyst: www.catalystwomen.org
- The National Network for Women's Employment: www.women work.org
- Small Business Administration's Online Women's Business Center: www.sba.gov/aboutsba/sbaprograms/onlinewbc/index .html
- The International Alliance for Women: www.tiaw.org
- National Partnership for Women and Families: www.national partnership.org

- National Association for Female Executives: www.nafe.com
- American Business Women's Association: www.abwahq.org
- 9to5, National Association of Working Women: www.9to5.org
- Center for Women's Business Research: www.cfwbr.org
- Break the Glass Ceiling: www.breaktheglassceiling.com

RESEARCH

- To help you with figuring out your salary, go to www.salary.com.
- To help find your perfect new town, go to www.findyourspot.com.
- To help you find the perfect house in the perfect new town, go to www.realtor.com.

SOCIAL NETWORKING

- www.myspace.com
- www.linkedin.com
- www.oomph.net

PRODUCTS

- www.seejanework.com
- www.staples.com

index

accomplishments, 8, 59, 179, 210. *See also* selling yourself
accountability, leadership and, 207
action plans, 31–32
administrative jobs, 62–63
Albright, Madeleine, 78
Alessandra, Tony, 53
anger, 135, 148–49. *See also* conflict
annual reviews, 146, 179, 180
appearance
    personal, 55, 109, 153–55, 167
    of résumés, 33
asking for what you deserve. *See* requests, making
authenticity, 70, 95–96, 203
autonomy, work styles and, 21, 29

being fired, 91, 103, 134–37
Bell, Kristen, 127
benefits, asking for, 186

Bengal, Wendy, 108, 168
Bernstein, Michelle, 104
Bevan, Peggy, 100
black-tie events, 167
Blackwell, Deborah, 171–72
blogs, 84, 85, 85–86, 165
Bohn, Holly, 79–80
book discussion groups, 67–68
boredom, assessing current career and, 15–16
bosses, 16, 75, 163, 184
    difficult, 102–3, 117–18
    fear of being, 100–102
    finding the power and, 157–58
    influencing upward, 161–62, 173
    job goals and, 24, 171–72
    negotiating and, 176–78
    selling yourself and, 63, 164
    signs of leaving, 134
bragging, 106, 175

Brierty, Linda, 189–91
Burke, Sarah, 155–56
business language, 151
business world, trends in, 200–204
Butterfield, Stewart, 83

career advancement. *See also*
        promotions
    bosses and, 161–62
    climbing the corporate ladder, 24
    flexible schedules and, 162–63, 182
    making requests and, 191
    men and, 175
    planning for, 160
career assessment
    boredom and, 15–16
    current career, 5, 6, 12–15
    past careers, 10–12
    picturing your ideal, 9–10
    work styles, 20–22
career changes, 13, 25–26, 39–40,
        172–73, 208
career counselors, 41
career planning
    action plans and, 31–32
    change and, 140
    entrepreneurship, 37–39
    examples of, 22–24, 43, 62
    job satisfaction and, 11
    long-term goals, 37, 213–15
    self-assessment and, 27–31
career timeline, 11–12
Catalyst, 17–18, 112–14
cell phones, 152, 153
challenges
    assessing current career and, 13
    building your professional profile,
        165
    career planning and, 214
    overcoming, 43
    positive thinking and, 58
    problem-solving, 195–97
    seeking more, 19
change. *See also* jobs, changing
    embracing, 78
    knowing when to make a, 39–40

losing your job and, 134–38
    preparing for, 132, 138–41
    signs of, 133–34
    at work, 16–17
Change Journey Coaching, 39
Charisma: Seven Keys to Developing the
        Magnetism that Leads to Success
        (Alessandra), 53
charters, teams and, 194
classes, taking. *See* education
clothing, 55, 109, 153–55, 167
Colabella, Chrisi, 49, 52–53, 77, 205,
        206
collaboration, teams and, 194
colleagues, 17, 29
    difficult, 103–5
    networking and, 71–72
    selling yourself and, 50
    success and, 8, 205
    your relationship with, 20, 147–48,
        168
commitment, teams and, 194
common areas, respecting, 153
communication, 89, 150–51
    with bosses, 161–62, 173
    with employees, 101, 198, 207
    office politics and, 146–47
    with possible mentors, 84–85
    problem-solving and, 195
    social events and, 167
    at staff meetings, 167–68
    teams and, 194
    tone of voice and, 94, 101, 109,
        120–21, 124, 156
communication networks, informal,
        17, 76
commutes, 182, 208
company needs
    asking for more staff, 183–84
    flexible schedules and, 181–82
    leadership and, 207
    making requests and, 175–76
    negotiating and, 176, 177–78, 179
    promotions and, 180–81
company policies, 16, 152, 181
competence, teams and, 194

concessions, negotiating and, 178
conferences and seminars, 68, 77, 166, 169, 186
confidence
    building, 173, 188–89
    entrepreneurship and, 38–39
    fears and, 93–96
    sales and, 60–61
    selling yourself and, 58, 64, 108, 109
conflict, 108, 148–49, 161, 173, 176, 191
consequences, teams and, 194
consulting business, 208–9
contacts, mentors and, 72–73, 82
control, teams and, 194
conversation, black-tie events and, 167
coordination, teams and, 194–95
coping skills, 118, 123–24, 130, 134–37
core workplace skills, 37
corporate retreats, 166–67
cost-of-living raises, 178, 180
coworkers. See colleagues
credibility, emotional responses and, 131
credit, 20, 103, 104–5, 158
crises, dealing with, 181–82
criticism, 19, 111–12, 124, 192
crying, 114–18, 124, 130, 210
cultural change, teams and, 195

delegating
    dealing with employees and, 100–101
    leadership and, 192, 193, 197–200, 206
    multitasking and, 102
    stereotyping and, 113
    trust and, 43
    vacations and, 185
Deussen, Christine, 182, 183
documenting problems, 196
dream job, envisioning, 41
dress codes. See clothing

education, 30, 79, 187
    changing professions and, 40

conferences and seminars, 68, 77, 166, 169, 186
    evolutionary leadership and, 203–4
    résumés and, 33
    sales training, 48–49
Eicher, Tiscia, 138–41, 199–200
elevator pitches, 56–58
e-mail, 109, 150–51, 163
emotional responses
    crying and, 114–18, 124, 130, 210
    making requests and, 191
    negotiating and, 176–77
    stereotyping and, 111–12
    taking things personally, 121–23, 177, 190
    to being laid off, 134–37
    women and, 128–31
emotional understanding, 24, 39
employees
    delegating and, 197–200
    empowerment of, 209
    fear of managing and, 100–102
    hiring, 170, 183–84, 206
    leadership and, 206–7
    problem-solving and, 195
    standing up for your, 156
    teams and, 193–95
    your relationship with, 22
empowerment, 209, 210–11
entrepreneurship, 37–39, 79–80, 138
etiquette, 151–53
evaluations. See annual reviews
evolutionary leadership, 202–4
expectations, team leadership and, 193, 207
expertise, 17, 58, 165, 203–4
eye contact, confidence and, 94

face-to-face contact, 71, 146–47, 182
Fake, Caterina, 82–86
faking confidence, 93–94
family responsibilities, 13, 14, 28, 93, 125, 169. See also work-life balance
Farnum, Andrea, 24–26

fears
    avoidance and, 96, 97
    confidence and, 93–96
    of flying, 89, 93
    of making requests, 175, 188–89,
        189–90
    of public speaking, 96–100
    recognizing, 89–93
    of your bosses, 102–3
    of your coworkers, 103–5
    of your employees, 100–102
Fiorina, Carly, 78
firing employees, 170
first impressions, 56–58, 109
flexible schedules, 7, 37–38, 181–83
flying, fear of, 89, 93
followups, selling yourself and, 52, 58

gender differences, in business, 2,
    111–14, 205, 214
General Motors (GM), 208
Girl's Guide to Being a Boss (Without
    Being a Bitch), The (Friedman and
    Yorio), 146
Girl's Guide to Starting Your Own
    Business, The (Friedman and
    Yorio), 39
glass ceilings, 190, 214
goals
    action plans and, 31–32
    career planning and, 28, 29–31
    fear of success and, 106
    goal statements, 53
    identifying, 9–10, 24, 193–94, 204
    long-term goals, 28, 37, 39–41, 53,
        54, 198
    raises and, 179
    selling yourself and, 53, 54, 59
Golden Seeds, 80–81
gossip, office politics and, 149–50
government, local, 68
grief, losing your job and, 134–37,
    137–38

Hart, Emily, 180
headhunters, 31, 180, 191

health, 123, 185
Heathfield, Susan, 193, 208–11
help, accepting, 38
hiring employees, 170, 183–84, 206
hobbies and interests, 29
honesty, 55, 95
humor, 95, 205

improvising, public speaking and, 98
industries, evaluating, 15–16, 30–31,
    32–33, 160
industry contacts, 72
industry standards, 168
influencing upward, 161–62, 173, 192,
    193
information access, 201–2
informational interviews, 15–16, 31,
    40
innovation, teams and, 194
insecurities. See fears
instant messaging, 150, 151
integrity, business and, 202–3
interruptions, 152
interviews, 15–16, 40, 50, 54–56, 210
interviews, with business women
    career paths, 22–26, 39–41, 41–43,
        62–65
    change and, 138–41
    fear and, 109–10
    gender differences and, 109–10,
        128–31
    influencing upward, 171–72, 172–73
    leadership, 205–7, 208–11
    making requests and, 188–89,
        189–91
    networking, 81–82, 82–86
    office politics and, 157–59
    selling yourself, 59–61, 62–65
introductions, public speaking and, 99

job descriptions, 169, 183
job losses
    being fired, 91, 103, 134–37
    layoffs, 16, 92–93, 133–34, 134–37,
        137–38, 170
    resigning and, 103

jobs, changing, 30–31. *See also* profession, changing
  action plans for, 31–32
  industry standards and, 168
  information access and, 201–2
  job search websites, 37
  knowing when to, 42–43, 133–34
  raises and, 179
job satisfaction
  assessing current career and, 6, 14–15
  boredom and, 15–16
  career planning and, 1–2
  difficult bosses and, 103
  embracing success and, 17
  past jobs and, 11–12
  positive thinking and, 107

Keating, Erin, 71–72
keywords, résumés and, 34
Kim Ricketts Book Events, 78
kindness, 24, 65
King, Billie Jean, 1
knowledge. *See* expertise
Kübler-Ross, Elisabeth, 135

labelling, emotional responses and, 131
LaFrance, Marianne, 115
languages, 42
lateness, chronic, 54–55
lateral moves, 64
Law of Attraction, 106
layoffs, 16, 92–93, 133–34, 134–37, 137–38, 170
leadership, 192, 205–7, 208–11
  defining success and, 7, 8
  delegating and, 197–200
  evaluating strengths and weaknesses, 19
  evolutionary leadership, 202–4
  fear of delegating and, 101
  problem-solving and, 195–97
  promotions and, 170
  raises and, 179
  stereotyping and, 112–13

supportiveness and, 118
teams and, 193–95
trends in, 200–204
women and, 17–18, 39, 79–81, 111–12
learning, ongoing, 19, 23, 38, 40, 81, 203–4. *See also* education
Lee, Jennifer, 39
life coaching, 39–41
Lish, Sandy, 109–10, 164, 180–81
listening skills, 52, 147, 149
loyalty, success and, 24, 191

MacGillivray, Lisa, 96–97
makeup, 155, 167
Malkin, Linda, 157–59
Malloy, Ellen, 16
management. *See also* bosses; leadership
  finding the power and, 157–58
  firing employees and, 91
  influencing upward, 161–62, 192, 193
  office conflicts and, 148–49
  your need for, 21
  your relationship with, 19
management, working in, 7, 17, 19, 92, 100–102
managing up. *See* influencing upward
mantras, career boosting, 9
meetings
  being left out of, 134
  contributing to, 19
  with employees, 207
  flexible schedules and, 182, 183
  speaking up at, 167–68
Mehleisen, Bill, 200–204
Melman-Smith, Karen, 114–15
men
  career advancement and, 47–48, 175
  clothing and, 153
  crying and, 116–17
  emotional responses and, 115–16, 120–21, 129–30, 210
  leadership and, 112–13
  networking and, 66, 67
mental health, 136, 185, 186

mentoring
   career assessment and, 19, 20
   emotional responses and, 112
   entertainment industry, 171
   fear of managing and, 100–101
   importance of, 65, 211, 214
   networking and, 70–71, 72–76,
     81–82
mentors, 43, 75–76, 84, 173, 205
mergers, 16
Miller, Kathleen, 188–89
Mills, Jess, 22–24
Minnihan, Erica Duignan, 80–81
modesty, barriers to success and, 109.
   See also bragging
money. *See* salaries
moodiness, 119–20
moonlighting, 12, 40
Moore, Mary Tyler, 126
Morrow, Liz, 122
motivations, 21, 23, 28, 29, 62, 132–33,
   206
moving up. *See* career advancement
multitasking, delegating and, 102

neatness, 152
negativity, 6, 27–28, 54, 94–95, 107,
   147–48
negotiating, 174, 176–78, 181–82,
   187–88. *See also* requests, making
networking, 29, 66–72, 77–81, 82–86,
   93, 198
   action plans and, 32
   building a network, 71–72
   changing jobs and, 31, 40, 42–43
   elevator pitches and, 56–57
   "how not to" lessons, 68–71
   mentoring and, 72–76, 81–82
   salaries and, 180
   selling yourself and, 51, 63
new job, acclimating to, 147
nonprofits, working at, 8

objectives
   résumés and, 32–33, 33–34
   selling yourself and, 50–51, 53–54

office politics, 19, 121, 145–46, 146–51,
   151–53, 156, 157–59
offices, 8, 152–53, 186–87
Old Boys' Club, 66
online communities, networking and,
   68
on-the-job training, 199
opportunities, leadership and, 195–97
Orman, Suze, 78, 99–100
Osbourne, Kelly, 80
overtime, working weekends, 162–63
overwork, 114–15, 123, 133, 184–85,
   191

Palone, Judy, 171
part-time work, 7, 183
passion, for work, 2, 7, 14–15, 20,
   95–96, 171–72, 205
peer pressure, career planning and, 28
Pennington, Josianne, 75–76
"people skills," difficult bosses and,
   103
performance reviews. *See* annual
   reviews
personal appearance, 55, 109, 153–55,
   167
personal belongings, respect for, 153
personal growth, negotiating and, 178
personal habits, interviews and, 55
personality, career and, 23–24, 29,
   110, 214, 215
personality tests, 29
personal life, 29, 40, 181–83. *See also*
   work-life balance
personal relationships, mentoring
   and, 73
perspective, maintaining, 121–23
phone etiquette, 109, 152, 152–53
PMS, 119–20
positional power, 113
positive thinking, 23, 58–59, 94–95,
   106–8. *See also* confidence
posture, confidence and, 94
power, finding, 157–58
PowerPoint presentations, 98
power struggles, 102

practicing, for difficult tasks, 51, 99, 176
premenstrual dysphoric disorder
  (PMDD), 119
Prime, Jeanine, 113
Prindible, Tara, 18
prioritizing, 32, 124, 133
privacy, crying and, 118
problem-solving, 113, 156, 195–97,
  202–3
procrastination, career planning and,
  28
productivity, working weekends and,
  162
profession, changing, 31, 40, 168. *See
  also* jobs, changing
professionalism, 24, 83–84
professional organizations, 51, 68, 77,
  82, 86, 186. *See also* networking
professional profile, building, 164–65
professional standards, 23–24
programs, developing, 165
promotions, 164, 169–71, 177
  asking for, 174, 175, 180–81, 187
  selling yourself and, 48, 64, 160
proposals, raises and, 179
publicity, 48, 179
public speaking, 89, 90–91, 96–100,
  170, 214

question and answer sessions, 98

Rackham, Neil, 50
Rainy, Allison, 169
raises, 169–70, 174, 175, 178–80, 187.
  See also salaries
Ramos, Jen, 11–12
references, 55
referrals, 52, 70–71
Regniault, Marcella, 62–65
rejection, 91–92, 186–88, 191
relationships, interpersonal
  difficult coworkers and, 103–5
  fear of being disliked and, 90
  networking and, 70–71, 86
  stereotypes and, 112–13
  "taking things personally," 122–23

relocating, 14, 31, 125, 169
reorganizations, 16, 134
reputation, at work, 50, 61, 63, 64,
  164–65, 180, 210
requests, making, 2, 51, 174, 175–76,
  189–91, 214
  asking for a flexible work schedule,
    181–83
  asking for a promotion, 180–81
  asking for a raise, 178–80
  asking for a vacation, 184–86
  asking for more staff, 183–84
  fear of, 188–89
  negotiating and, 176–78
  rejection and, 58–59, 91–92,
    186–88
research, 40, 55, 84–85, 97
resentment, success and, 190–91
resigning, 103
resources, utilizing, 198, 199
respect, at work, 187
responsibilities, taking on, 164, 170,
  194, 199
résumés, 31–32, 32–36, 49–50
rewards, for employees, 206
Rhimes, Shonda, 126
Ricketts, Kim, 78
risk management, 157
Rockmore, Alicia, 14–15
Roffey Park, 145
role models, for women, 39
role playing. *See* practicing
Rosen, Andrea, 122
routines, leadership and, 199–200
rules, business success and. *See*
  professional standards
ruts, professional, 24, 26

salaries
  career assessment and, 13, 30
  family responsibilities and, 14
  job satisfaction and, 7
  as motivators, 21, 25, 132–33
  promotions and, 169, 169–70
  raises and, 169–70, 174, 175,
    178–80, 187

schedules, 7, 21, 37–38, 181–83
Schiffman, Steve, 50
science, of crying, 116
Scura, Jeanne Marie, 59–61
"Secret, The," 106
self-assessment
    career changes and, 26, 140–41
    career planning and, 27–31, 213–14
    defining success and, 7–8
    elevator pitches and, 56–57
    envisioning your dream job, 41
    evaluating strengths and
        weaknesses, 18–20
    work styles, 20–22
self-care, 40
self employment, travel and, 93
self-esteem. See confidence
Self-Inquiry Process, The (Brierty), 189
selling yourself, 47–58, 108, 163,
        175–76, 205
    building your professional profile,
        164–65
    influencing upward, 161–62
    in interviews, 210
    mentors and, 76
    résumés and, 32
setting objectives, career planning
        and, 31–32
sharing your story, 77–78, 99–100, 205
Sherman, Lynn, 186–87
Shields, Stephanie, 117, 128–31
shortcomings, facing your, 18–20
sincerity, confidence and, 95
skills, 29, 51, 170
    coping skills, 118, 123–24, 130,
        134–37
    core workplace skills, 37
    listening skills, 52, 147, 149
    résumés and, 33, 34
    updating, 14, 40, 187
Snyder, Cori, 137–38
social networking websites, 55, 76–77,
        83–84, 201, 201–2
social roles, women and, 189–90
social situations, career advancement
        and, 67–68, 76–77, 165–67

solutions, offering, 177, 196–97
speakerphones, 152
Speaking From the Heart: Gender and the
        Social Meaning of Emotion
        (Shields), 128
speaking up, at staff meetings, 167–68
Sperger, Charlene, 205–7
SPIN selling, 50
spiritual principles, career growth
        and, 9
sports, emotional responses and,
        129–30
staff. See employees
staff meetings. See meetings
status reports, vacations and, 184, 185
stay-at-home moms, 124–25, 205, 213
stereotyping, 128–31
    crying, 114–18
    leadership and, 112–13, 192–93
    PMS, 119–20
    "taking things personally," 121–23
    television and, 126–28
    tone of voice and, 120–21
    women and, 18, 111–14, 190
    working mothers and, 124–25
Stewart, Martha, 82, 116
stories, sharing. See sharing your story
strengths and weaknesses, evaluating,
        18–20
stress, 7, 21, 96, 116, 123–24, 145–46,
        153, 184–85
success
    barriers to, 109–10
    of colleagues, 205
    defining, 6, 7–8, 9–10, 205
    fear of, 106
    strategies for, 17–18
    for women, 23–24
Summary of Qualifications, résumés
        and, 3, 34
supportiveness, women and, 112–13,
        118, 158–59, 168
support systems, 67–68, 141

taking things personally, 121–23, 177,
        190

teams, 192, 193, 193–95, 199–200, 210. *See also* leadership
teamwork, 29, 181, 206
technology industry, updating skills and, 14
telecommuting, 182
television, stereotyping and, 126–28
tempers, 94, 124, 149
temp work, 183
thank-you notes, 52, 151
theft, 102–3
Thomas, Marlo, 126
Thurber, Marshall, 201
time-management, 30, 54–55, 162, 197–200
timing, making requests and, 178, 179–80
titles, 7, 181
tone of voice, 94, 101, 109, 120–21, 124, 156
trademarks, 195–96
trade publications, 31, 165, 180
training, on the job, 199
travel, 7, 93, 139, 140, 169, 200
trends, watching, 37
triggers, crying and, 118, 130
trust, 141, 147–48, 198, 203
tuition reimbursement, 187

undermining yourself, emotional responses and, 131

vacations, asking for, 184–86, 187
values, career planning and, 30
venture capital firms, for women, 80–81

voice mail greetings, 109
volunteering, 40, 42, 165

Walker, Megan, 179
websites
    career sites, 32, 34, 37, 115–16, 180, 184
    informational sites, 85
    social networking sites, 55, 76–77, 83–84
Winfrey, Oprah, 82
win-win negotiations, 176
Women "Take Care," Men "Take Charge" (Catalyst), 112
Words Can Heal, 149–50
workforce. *See* employees
work history, 10–12, 33
working from home. *See* telecommuting
working mothers, 7, 124–25, 200
working weekends, 162–63
work-life balance, 2, 205
    commutes and, 208
    flexible schedules and, 181–83
    job satisfaction and, 7, 11
    maintaining perspective and, 122
    overwork and, 133
    working mothers and, 78, 124–25
workspaces. *See* offices
work styles, 17, 20–22, 29
Wu, Vicky S., 76, 81–82

yelling. *See* tone of voice
Yorio, Sharyn, 151